RECORDED VERSIONS
GUITAR
AUTHENTIC TRANSCRIPTIONS
WITH NOTES AND TABLATURE

CHRISTIAN
ACOUSTIC GUITAR HITS

ISBN 978-1-4234-3459-7

HAL•LEONARD®
CORPORATION
7777 W. BLUEMOUND RD. P.O. BOX 13819 MILWAUKEE, WI 53213

Visit Hal Leonard Online at
www.halleonard.com

All I Really Want

Words and Music by Lincoln Brewster

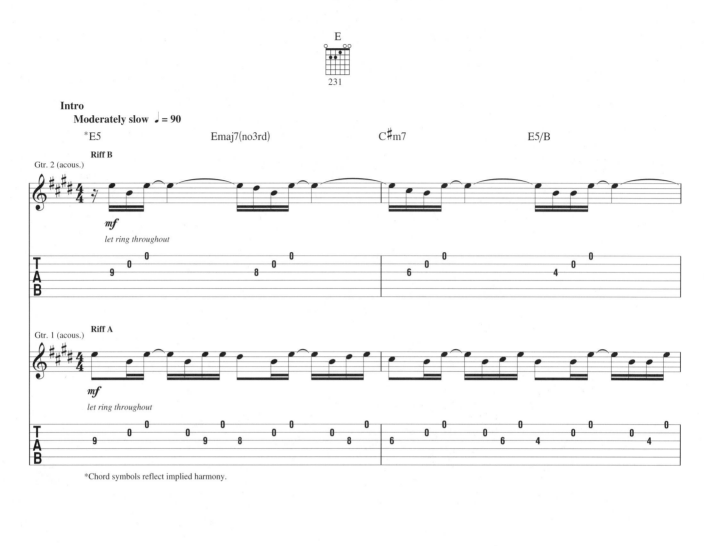

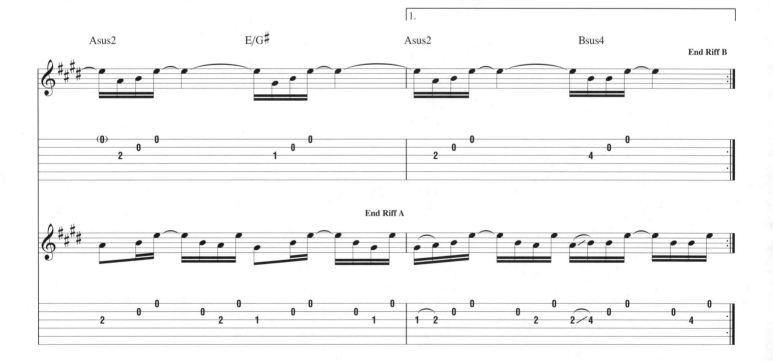

*Chord symbols reflect implied harmony.

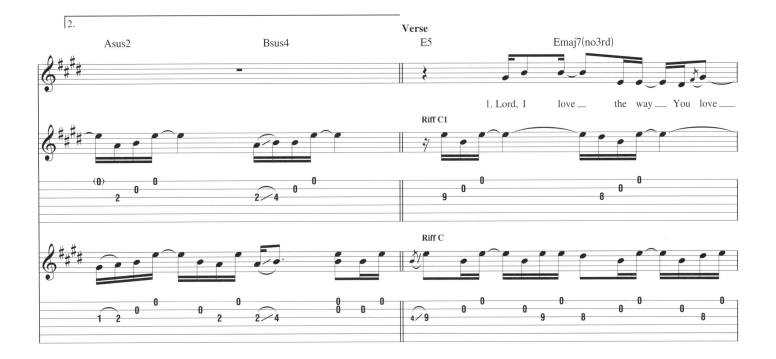

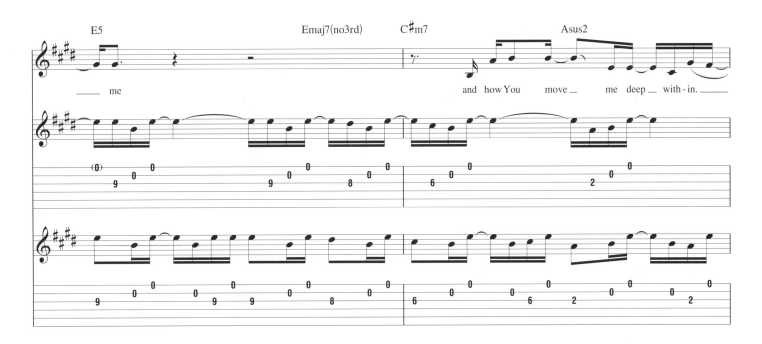

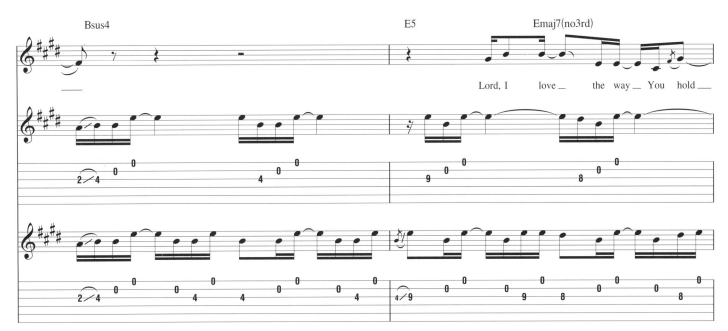

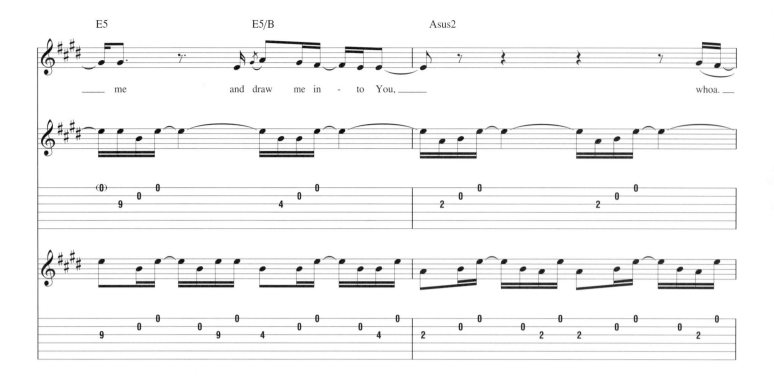

Gtrs. 1 & 2: w/ Riffs C & C1

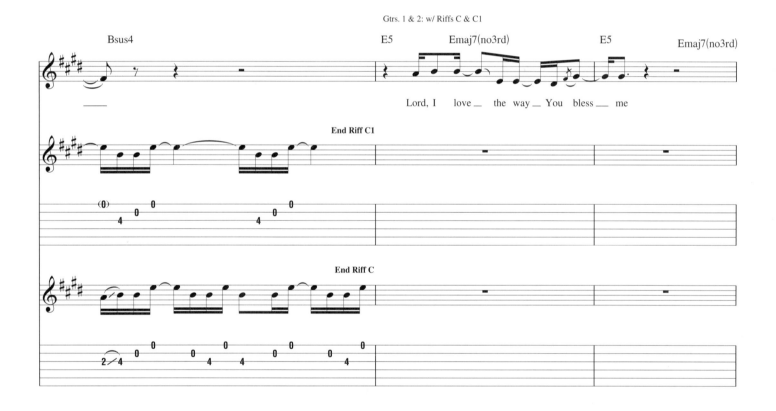

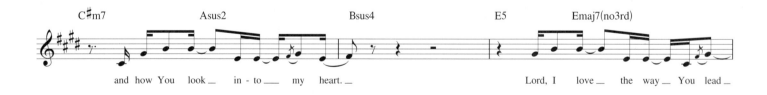

Chorus

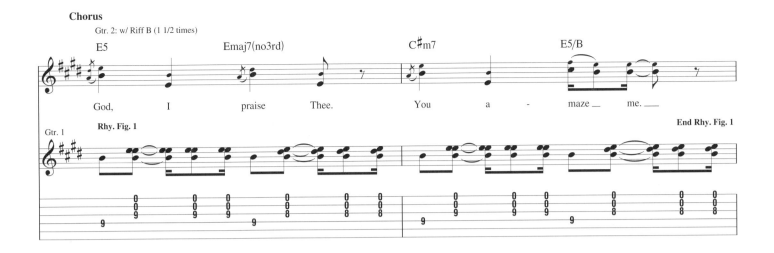

God, I praise Thee. You a- maze me.

Take my life and let Your light shine through.

Je- sus, Sav- ior, Friend of sin- ners,

fill me up 'cause all I real- ly want is more of You.

Interlude

You. (La, da, da, da, oh, whoa, oh, whoa, whoa, ah.)

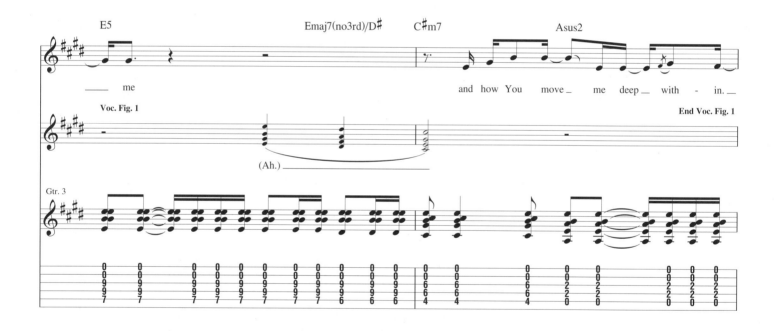

me and draw me in - to You, ____ whoa.

(Ah.)

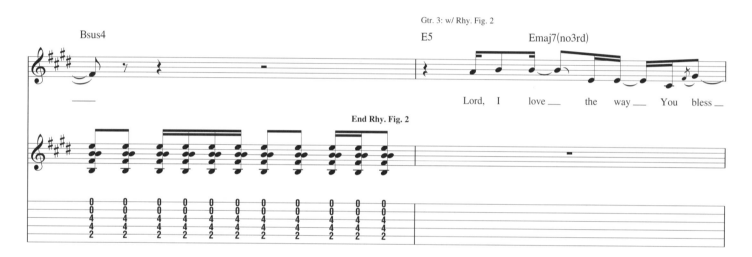

Gtr. 3: w/ Rhy. Fig. 2

Bsus4   E5   Emaj7(no3rd)

____ Lord, I love ____ the way ____ You bless ____

End Rhy. Fig. 2

Bkgd. Voc.: w/ Voc. Fig. 1

E5   Emaj7(no3rd)/D♯   C♯m7   Asus2

____ me,   oh, ____ and how You look ____ in - to ____ my heart. ____

Bsus4   E5   Emaj7(no3rd)

____ And, Lord, I love ____ the way ____ You lead ____

E5   E5/B   Asus2   Bsus4

____ me right in - to ____ Your ____ arms, ____ yeah,   whoa. ____

(Ah.)

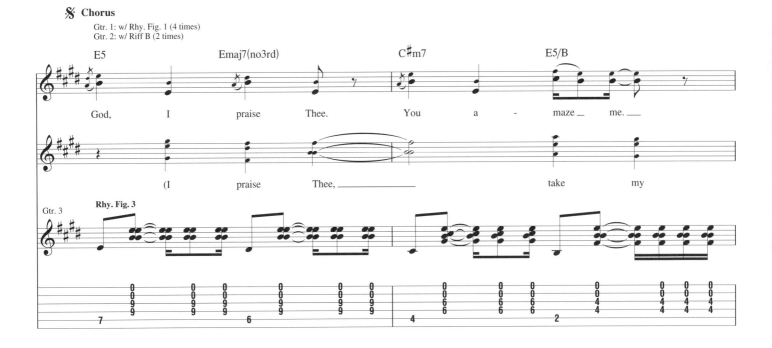

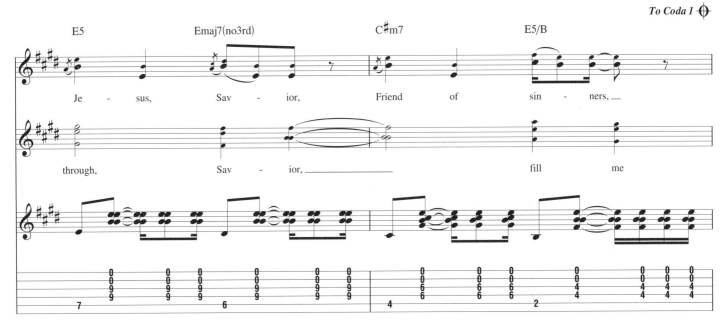

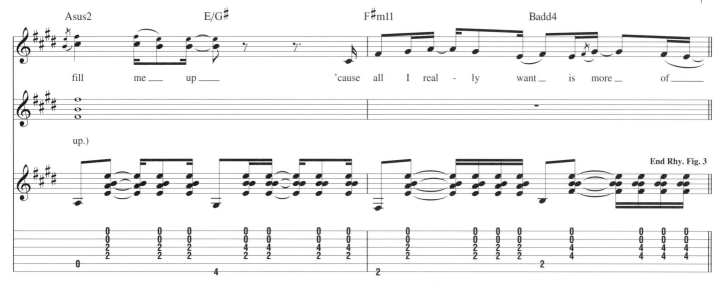

fill me — up — 'cause all I real - ly want — is more — of —

(up.)

End Rhy. Fig. 3

Interlude

Gtr. 1: w/ Riff A
Gtr. 2: w/ Riff B (1st 3 meas.)
Gtr. 3: w/ Rhy. Fig. 3 (1st 3 meas.)

— You.

(La, da, da, da, — oh, — whoa, oh, whoa, whoa, — ah.) —

Bridge

Gtr. 3 tacet

*E   F#m11   E/G#   Asus2

(La, da, — la, da, — la, — la, da, —

Gtr. 2

Gtr. 1

Gtr. 3

*Chord symbols reflect overall harmony.

11

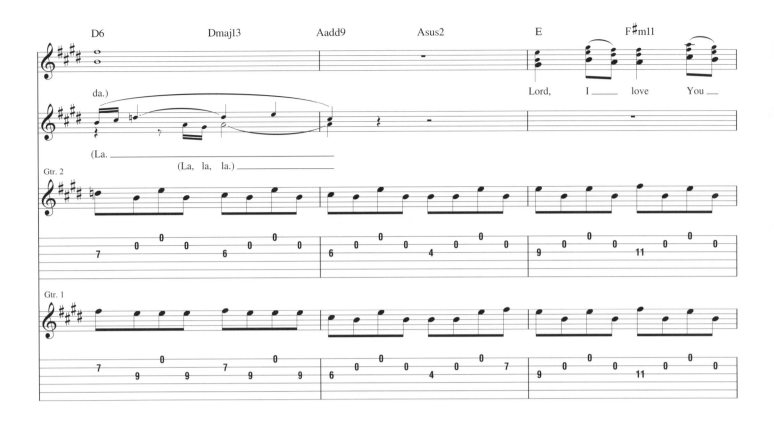

D.S. al Coda 1

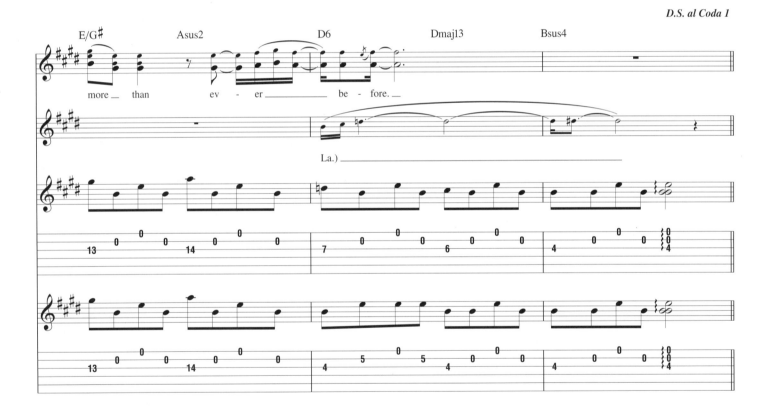

Coda 1

D.S. al Coda 2

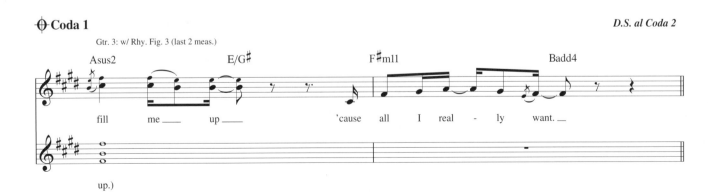

⊕ **Coda 2**

Gtr. 1: w/ Rhy. Fig. 1 (6 times)
Gtr. 2: w/ Riff B (3 times)
Gtr. 3: w/ Rhy. Fig. 3 (1 1/2 times)

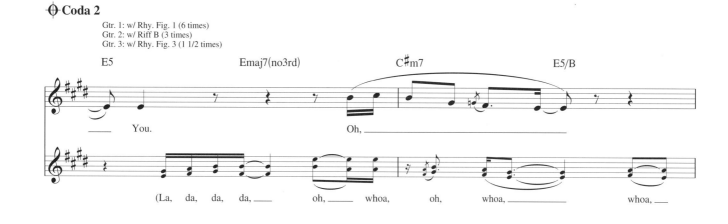

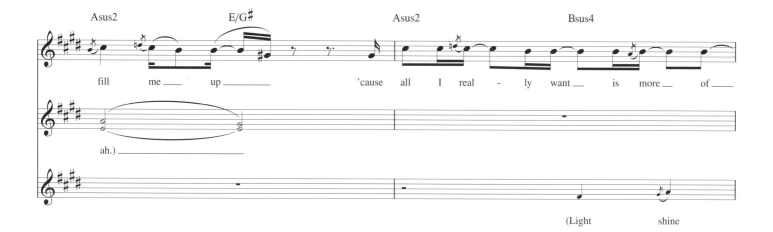

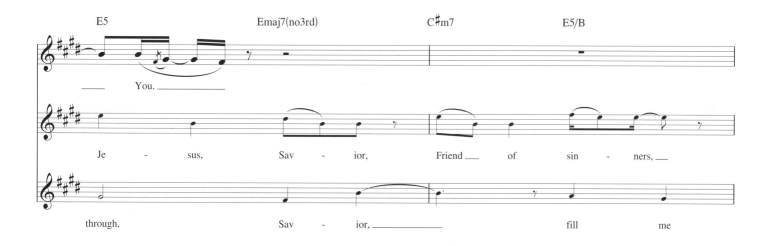

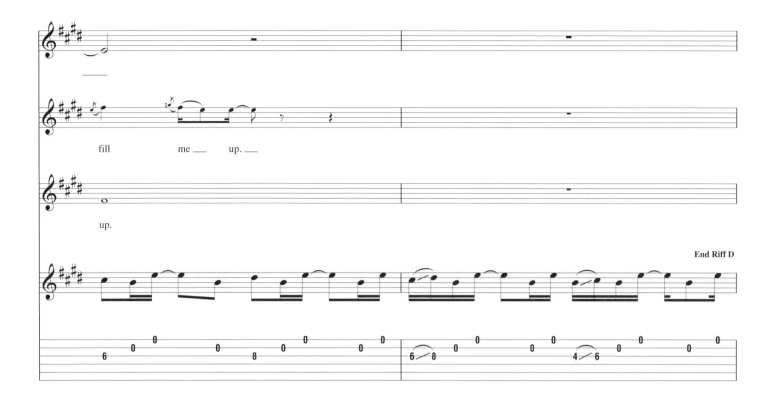

fill　　　me ___ up. ___

up.

End Riff D

Gtrs. 1 & 2: w/ Riff D (3 1/2 times)

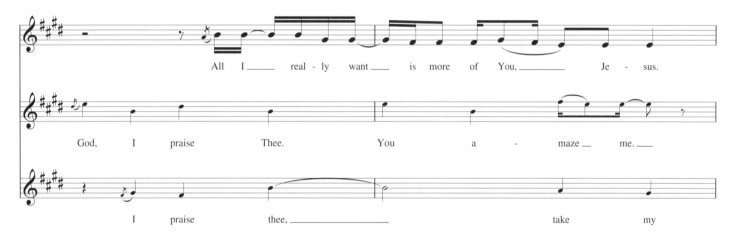

All I ___ real - ly want ___ is more of You, _____ Je - sus.

God, I praise Thee. You a - maze ___ me. ___

I praise thee, _____ take my

Come ___ and fill ___ me ___ up. ___

Take my ___ life. ___ Je - sus, Sav - ior,

life. Light shine through, Sav - ior, ___

Oh, _____ yeah, yeah. __ You're all I

Friend of sin - ners, __ fill me up. __

____ fill me up.

real - ly want. __ Oh, _____ I love ___ the way, _____ the

God, I praise Thee. You a - maze __ me. __

I praise Thee, _____ take my

way You love __ me. __

Take my life. __ Je - sus, Sav - ior,

life. Light shine through, Sav - ior, _____

Friend of sin - ners, ___ fill me _____ up.) ____

____ fill me _____ up.)

Dare You to Move

Words and Music by Jonathan Foreman

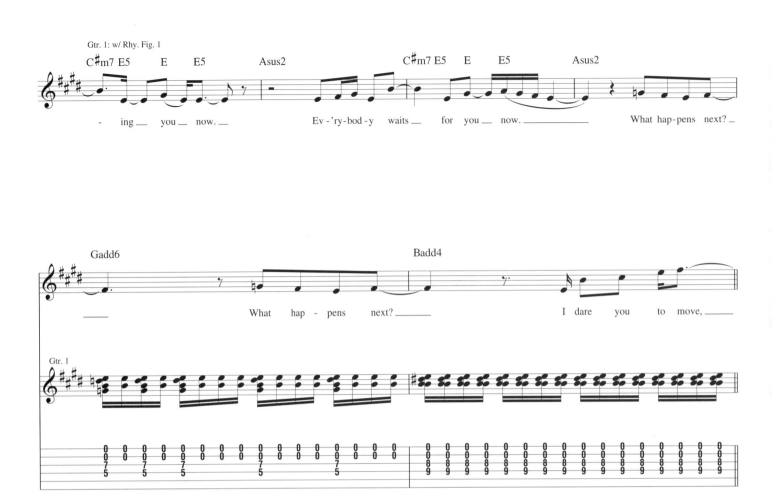

Gtr. 1: w/ Rhy. Fig. 1

C#m7 E5   E   E5   Asus2   C#m7 E5   E   E5   Asus2

-ing __ you __ now. __   Ev-'ry-bod-y waits __ for you __ now. ____   What hap-pens next?

Gadd6   Badd4

___   What hap-pens next? ____   I dare   you   to move, ____

Gtr. 1

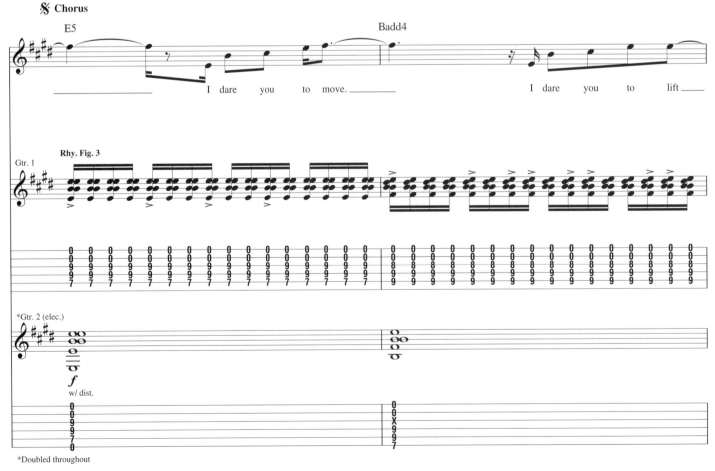

𝄋 **Chorus**

E5   Badd4

____   I dare   you   to move. ____   I dare you to lift ____

Gtr. 1

Rhy. Fig. 3

*Gtr. 2 (elec.)

𝆑
w/ dist.

*Doubled throughout

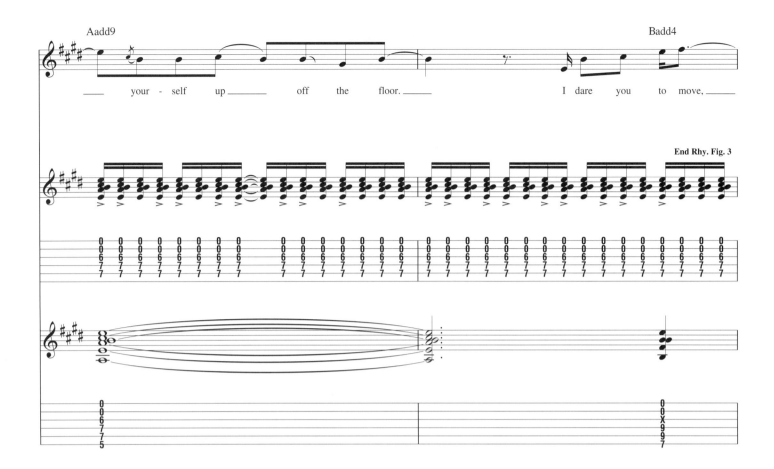

your - self up _____ off the floor. _____ I dare you to move, _____

End Rhy. Fig. 3

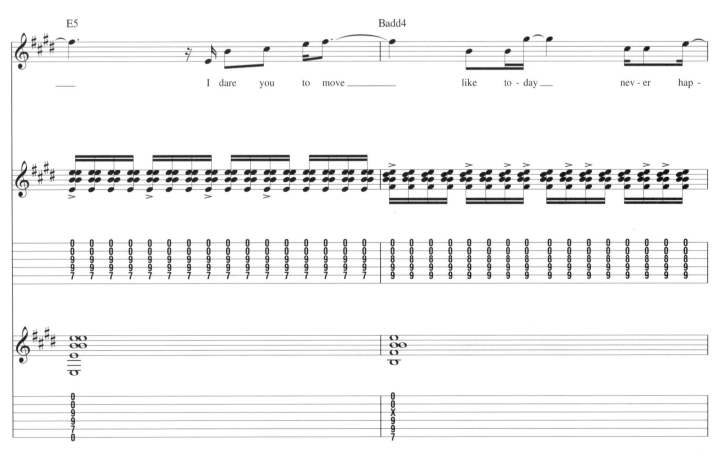

I dare you to move _____ like to - day _____ nev - er hap -

*Harmonic is produced by laying L.H. index finger
across 7th fret in an effort to stop the sound.

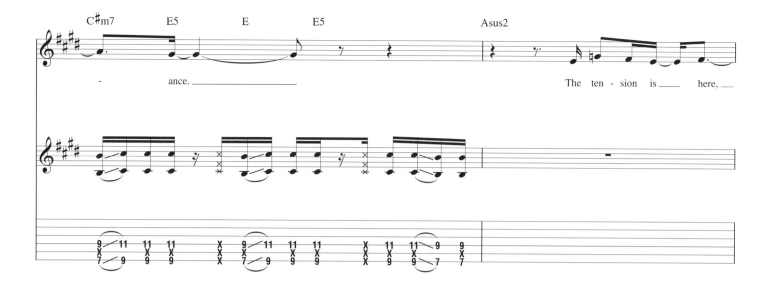

-ance. _____ The ten - sion is ____ here, ___

Gtr. 1: w/ Rhy. Fig. 2

____ the ten - sion is ____ here _____ be -tween who __ you are ___

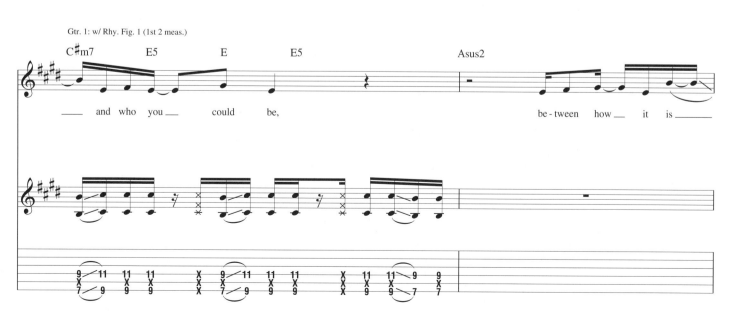

Gtr. 1: w/ Rhy. Fig. 1 (1st 2 meas.)

____ and who you ___ could be, be - tween how __ it is _____

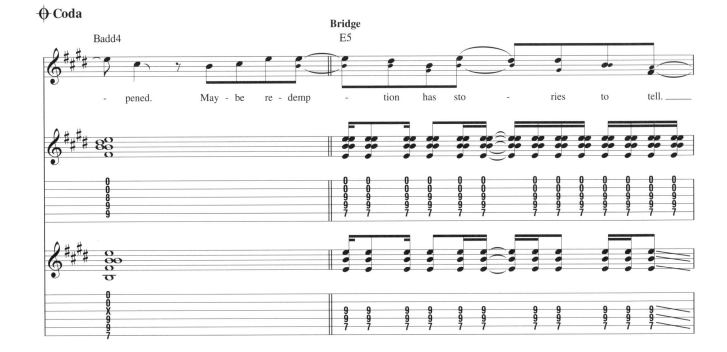

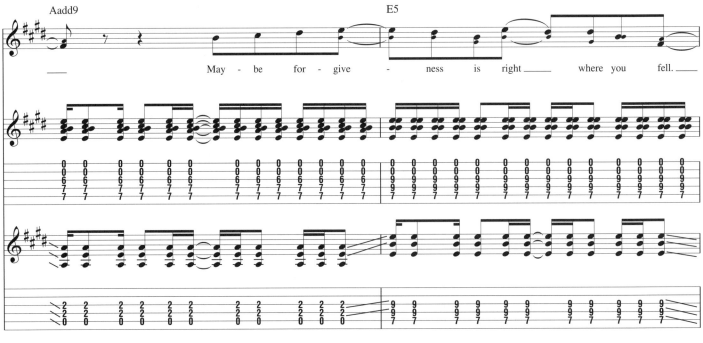

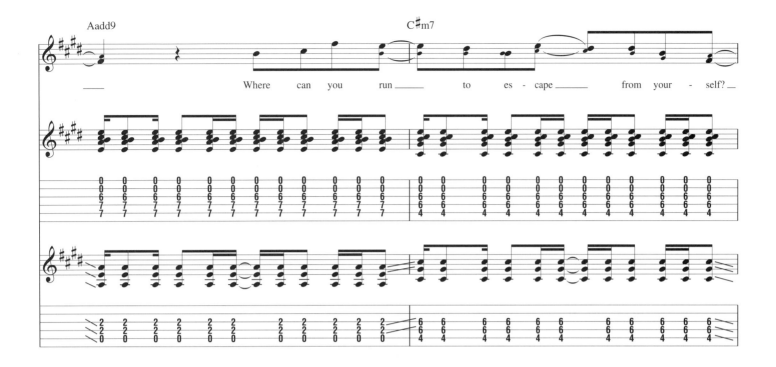

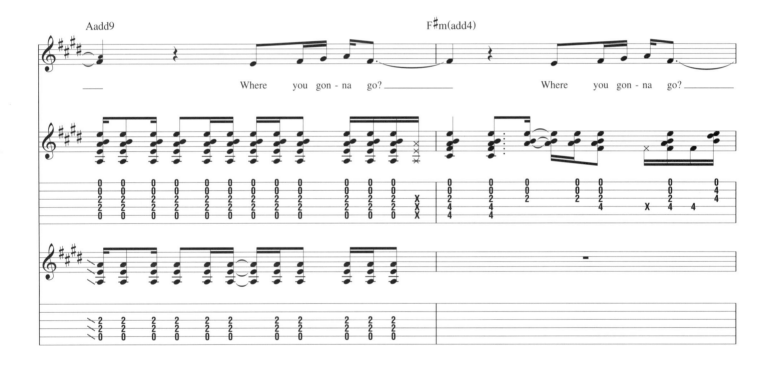

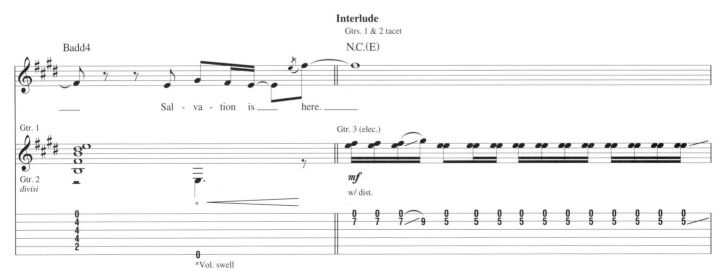

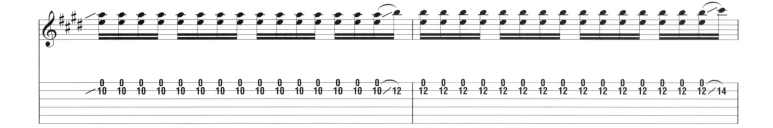

Outro-Chorus

Gtr. 1: w/ Rhy. Fig. 3 (1 1/2 times)
Gtr. 3 tacet

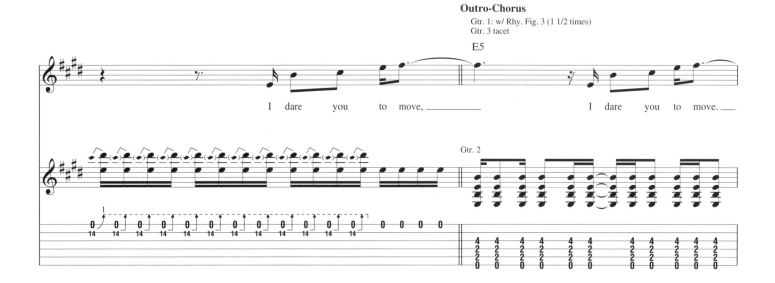

I dare you to move, _____ I dare you to move. __

Gtr. 2

I dare you to lift _____ your-self, ___ lift your-self up off the

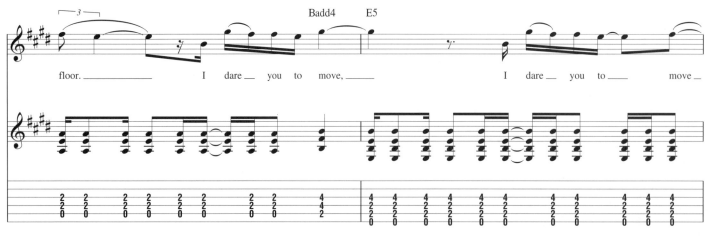

floor. _____ I dare __ you to move, _____ I dare __ you to ___ move

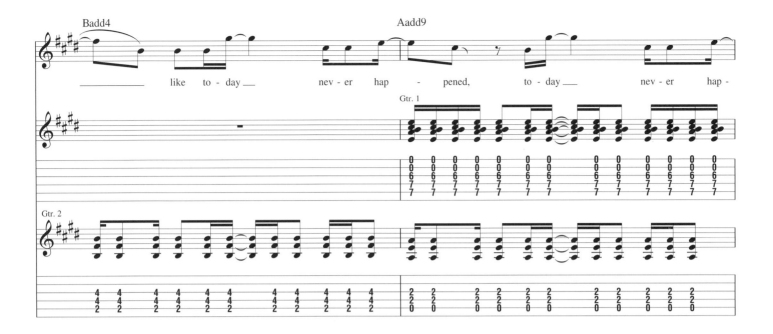

like to - day ____ nev - er hap - pened, to - day ____ nev - er hap -

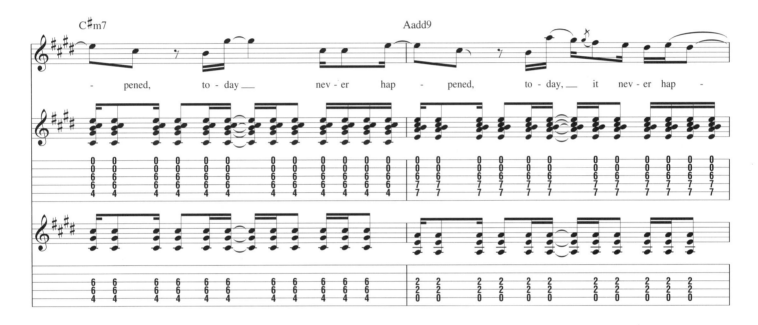

- pened, to - day ____ nev - er hap - pened, to - day, ____ it nev - er hap -

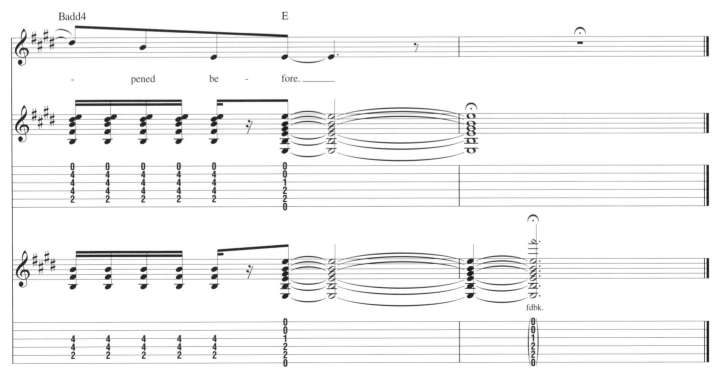

- pened be - fore. ____

Flood

Words and Music by Charlie Lowell, Dan Haseltine, Matt Odmark and Stephen Mason

His Eyes

Words and Music by Steven Curtis Chapman and James Isaac Elliott

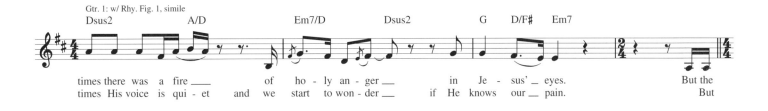

Gtr. 1: w/ Rhy. Fig. 1, simile

| Dsus2 | A/D | Em7/D | Dsus2 | G | D/F# | Em7 |

times there was a fire ___ of ho - ly an - ger ___ in Je - sus' _ eyes. But the
times His voice is qui - et and we start to won - der ___ if He knows our _ pain. But

Pre-Chorus

| Asus4 | A7 | D5 | D | A/C# |

eyes that _ saw hope _ in the hope - less, that
He who _ spoke peace to the wa - ter, cares

Gtr. 1

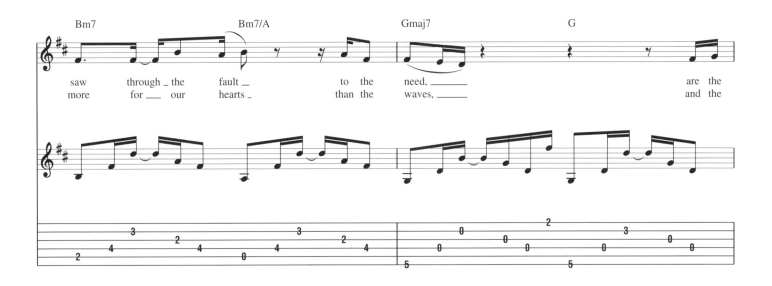

| Bm7 | Bm7/A | Gmaj7 | G |

saw through _ the fault _ to the need, _____ are the
more for _ our hearts _ than the waves, _____ and the

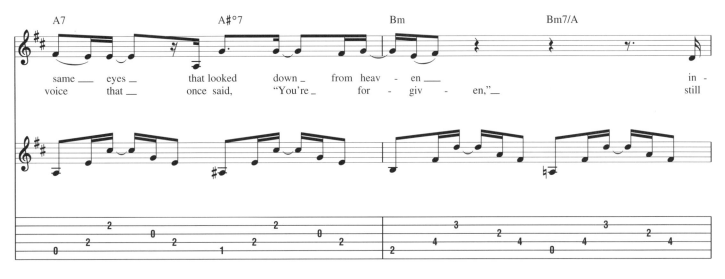

| A7 | A#°7 | Bm | Bm7/A |

same _ eyes _ that looked down _ from heav - en ___ in -
voice that _ once said, "You're _ for - giv - en,"_ still

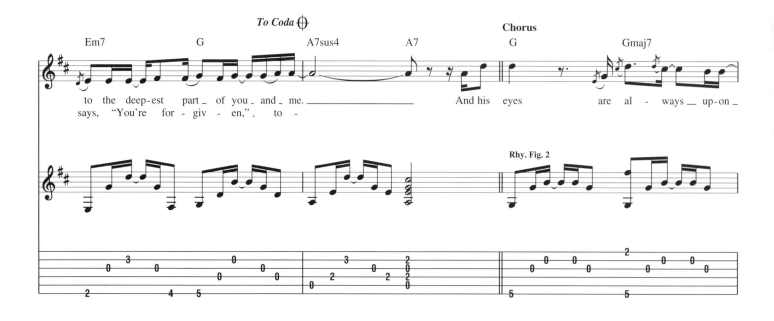

Holy Is the Lord

Words and Music by Chris Tomlin and Louie Giglio

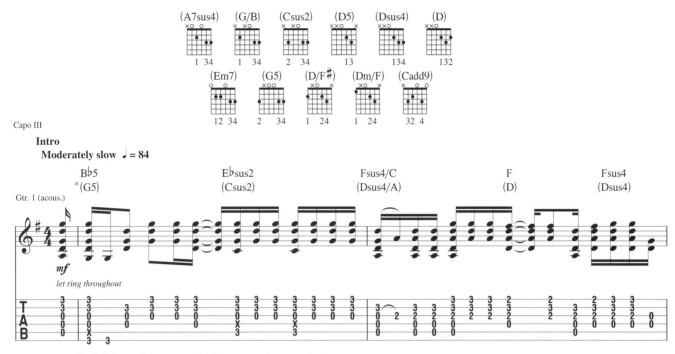

Capo III

Intro
Moderately slow ♩ = 84

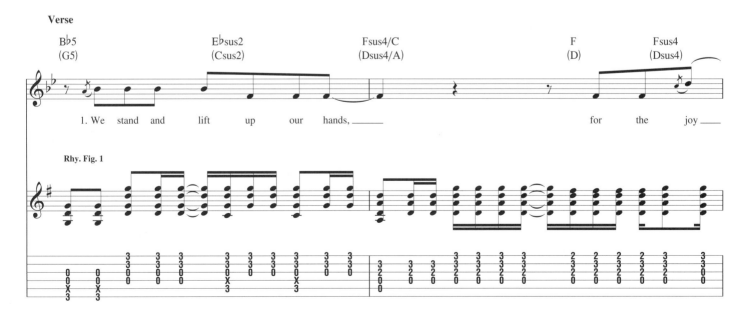

*Symbols in parentheses represent chord names respective to capoed guitar.
Symbols above reflect actual sounding chords. Capoed fret is "0" in tab.

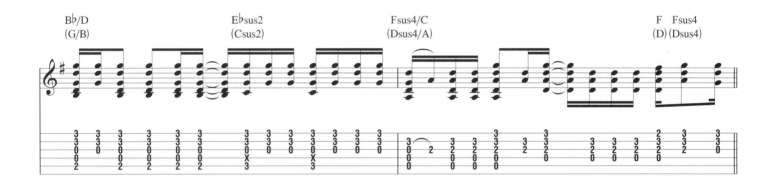

Verse

1. We stand and lift up our hands, _____ for the joy _____

Rhy. Fig. 1

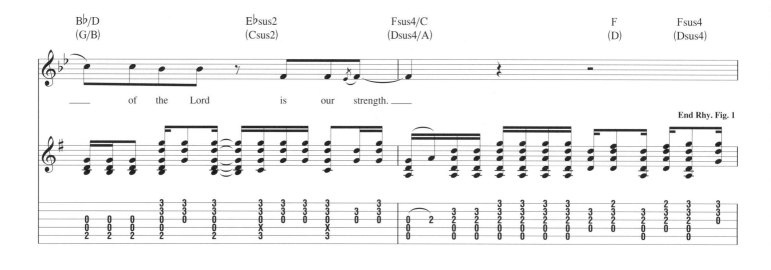

of the Lord   is   our   strength.

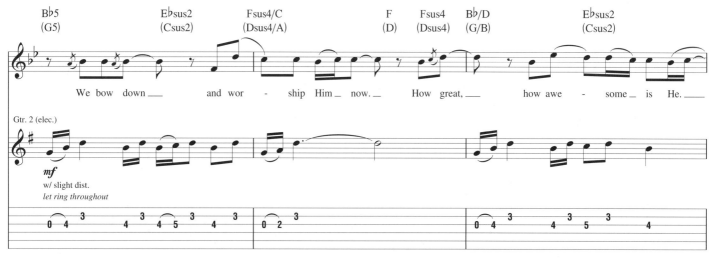

We bow down ___   and wor - ship Him _ now. _ How great, ___   how awe - some _ is He. ___

___ And to - geth - er we _ sing. ___   Ho - ly is ___ the Lord _

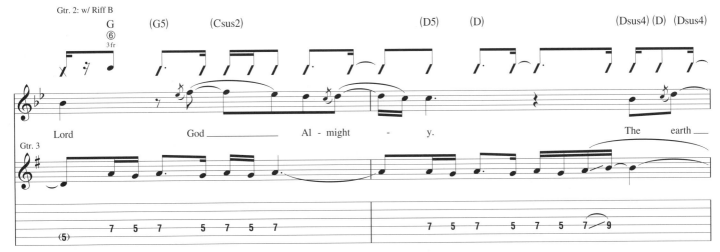

is filled ____ with His glo - ry. The earth ____

is filled ____ with His glo - ry. ____

Verse

Gtr. 1: w/ Rhy. Fig. 1 (1 1/2 times)

2. We stand and lift up our hands, ____ for the joy ____ of the Lord is our strength. ____

Chorus

Gtr. 1: w/ Rhy. Fig. 3
Gtr. 2: w/ Riff B (2 times)
Gtr. 3: w/ Riff C

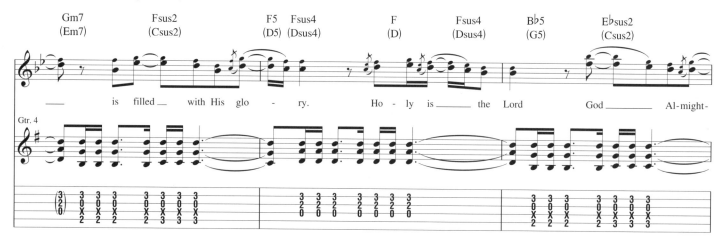

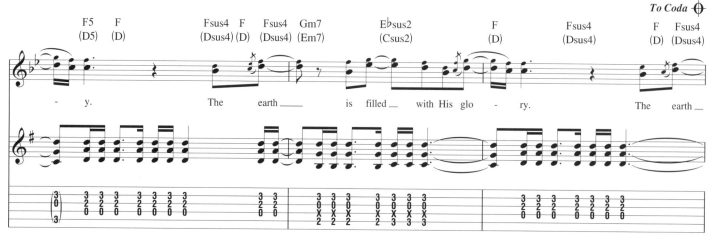

Gtr. 2: w/ Riff B (last 2 meas.)

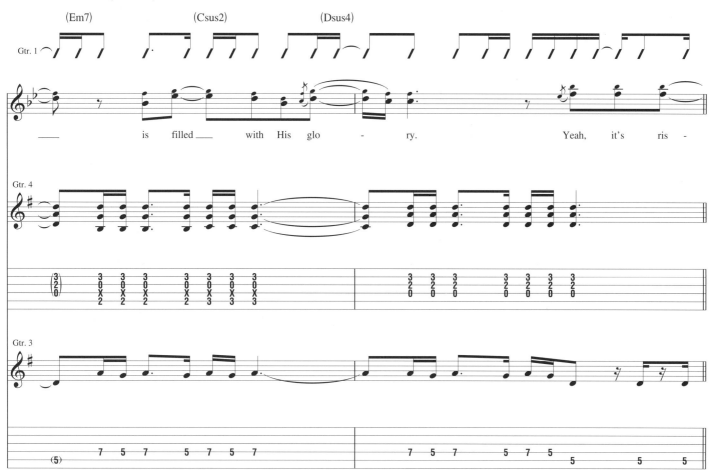

is filled ___ with His glo - ry. Yeah, it's ris -

Bridge

Gtr. 3 tacet

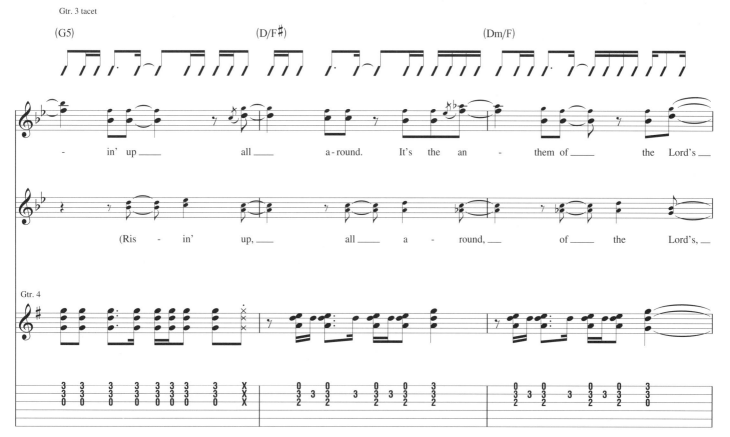

- in' up ___ all ___ a - round. It's the an - them of ___ the Lord's ___

(Ris - in' up, ___ all ___ a - round, ___ of ___ the Lord's, ___

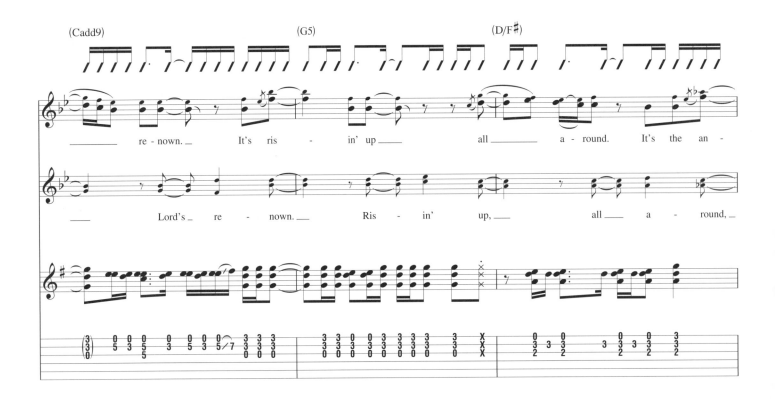

⊕ Coda

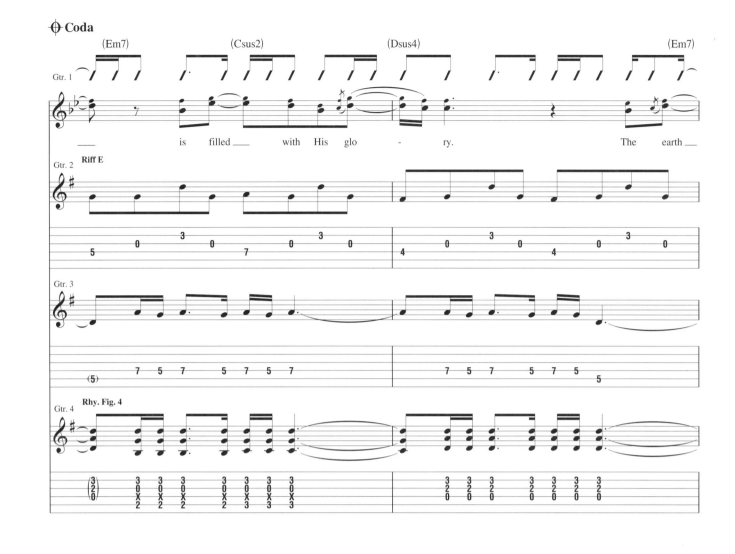

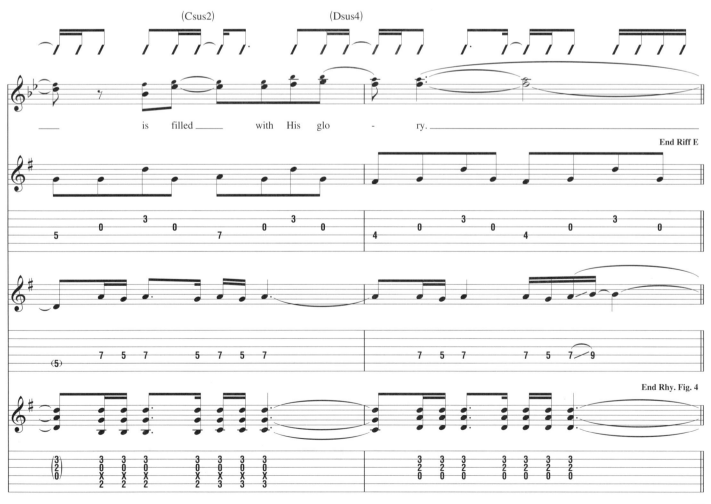

Interlude

Gtr. 2: w/ Riff E (till fade)
Gtr. 4: w/ Rhy. Fig. 4 (till fade)

(Em7) (Csus2) (D)

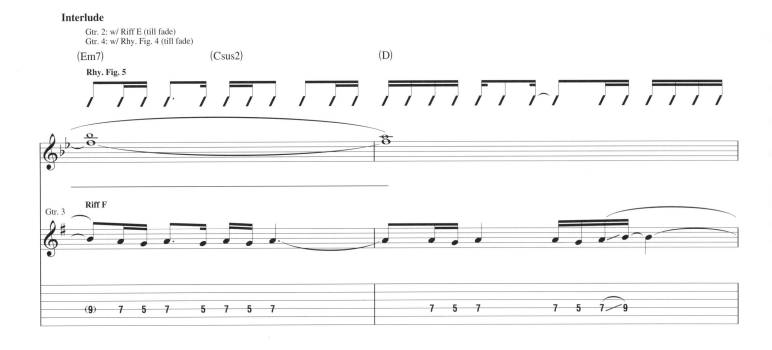

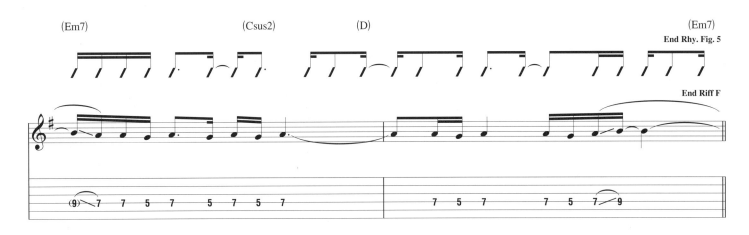

Outro

Gtr. 1: w/ Rhy. Fig. 5 (till fade)
Gtr. 3: w/ Riff F (till fade)

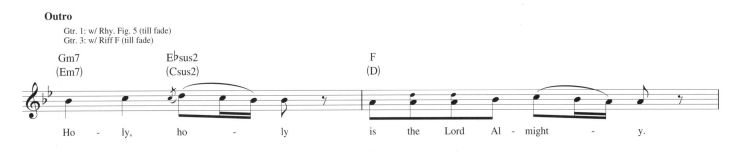

Ho - ly, ho - ly   is   the   Lord   Al - might - y.

2nd time, begin fade

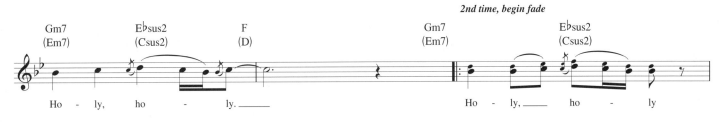

Ho - ly, ho - ly. _____   Ho - ly, _____ ho - ly

2nd time, fade out

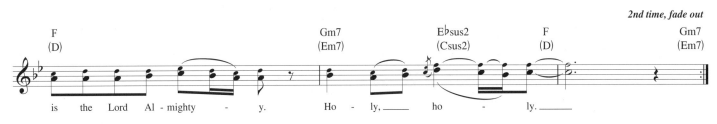

is   the   Lord   Al - mighty - y.   Ho - ly, _____ ho - ly. _____

I Could Sing of Your Love Forever

Words and Music by Martin Smith

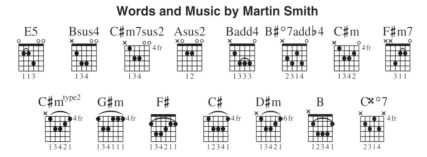

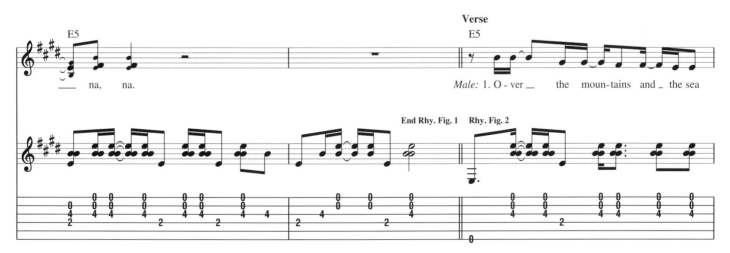

*w/ echo repeats

Interlude-Chorus

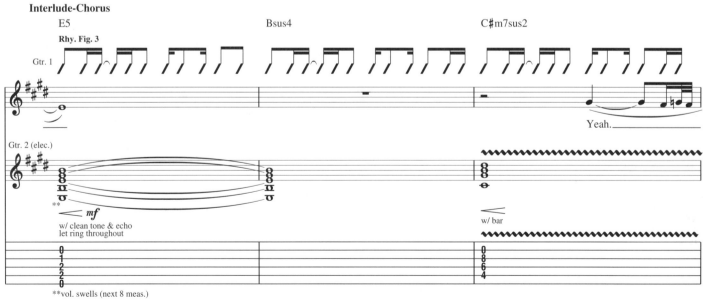

**vol. swells (next 8 meas.)

*w/ echo repeats

End Rhy. Fig. 3

Female: Oh, _____ yeah.

w/ bar

Gtr. 3 (elec.)

w/ slight dist.

P.M.

let ring _ _ _ _ _ _ _ _ _ _

let ring _ _ _ _ _ _ _ _ _

**w/ echo repeats

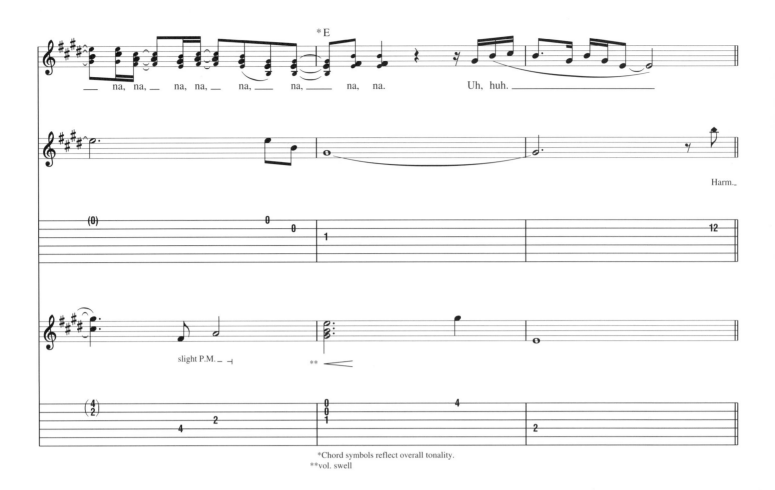

*Chord symbols reflect overall tonality.
**vol. swell

Verse

Gtr. 1: w/ Rhy. Fig. 2, simile

E5   G#m♭6

2. O - ver ___ the moun - tains and ___ the sea   your riv - er runs ___ with a love   for me.

Harm.

Riff A

P.M. -

†vol. swells (next 6 meas.)

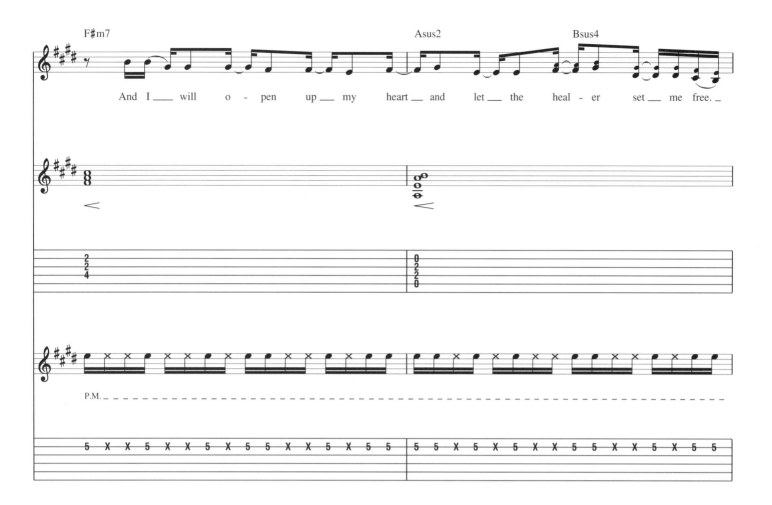

And I — will o - pen up — my heart — and let — the heal - er set — me free. —

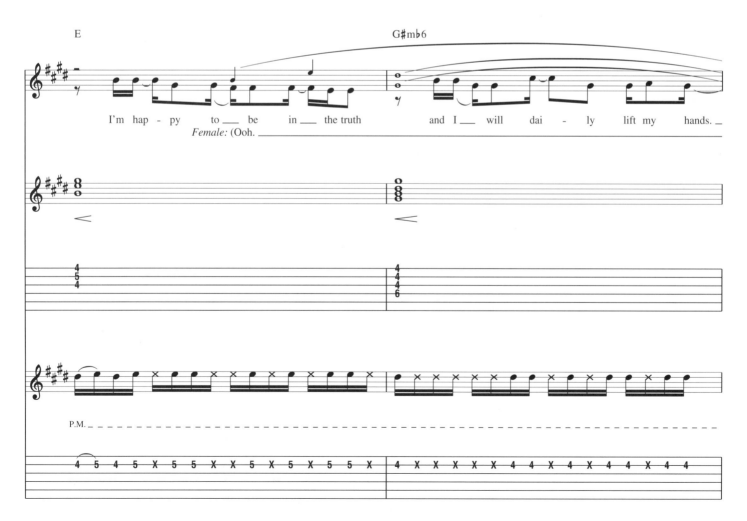

I'm hap - py to — be in — the truth and I — will dai - ly lift my hands. —

Female: (Ooh. —

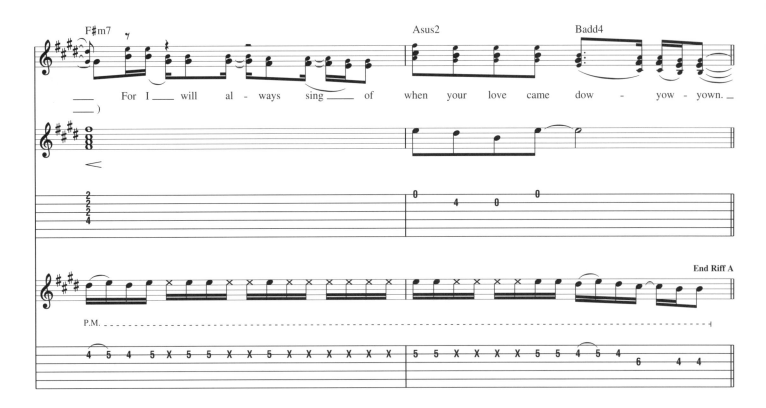

Chorus

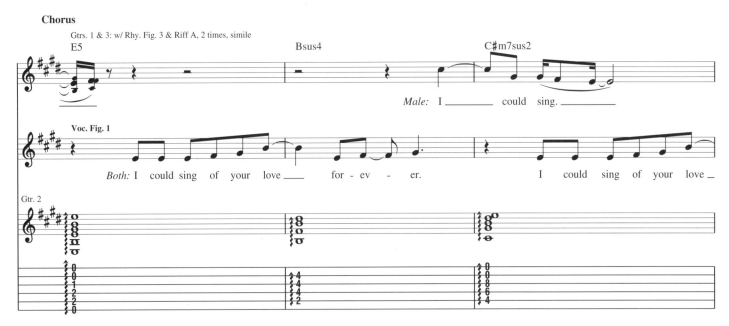

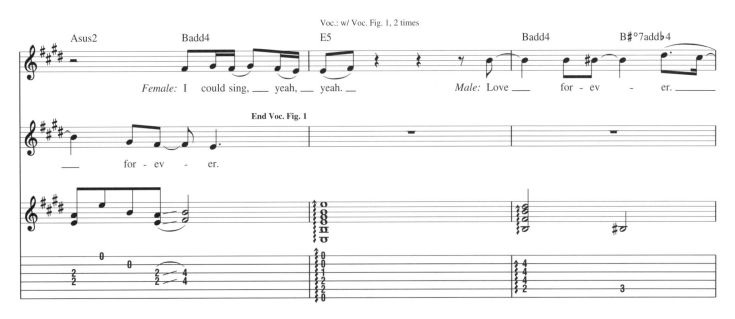

Bridge

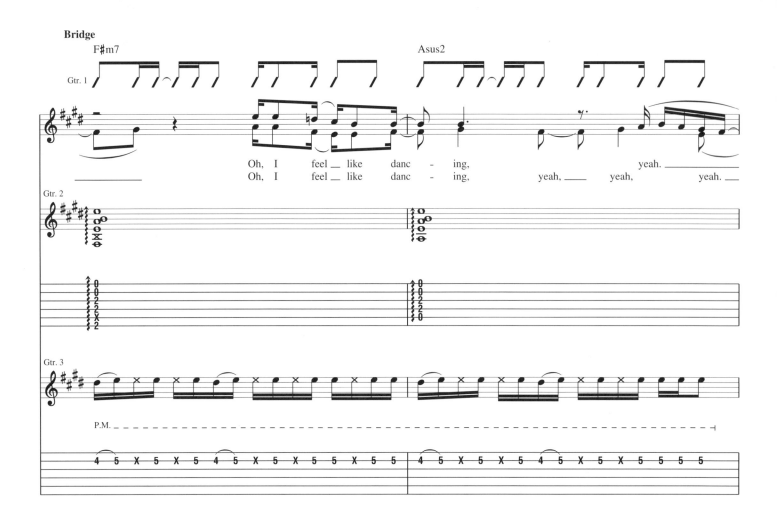

Oh, I feel __ like danc __ - ing, yeah. __
Oh, I feel __ like danc __ - ing, yeah, __ yeah, __ yeah. __

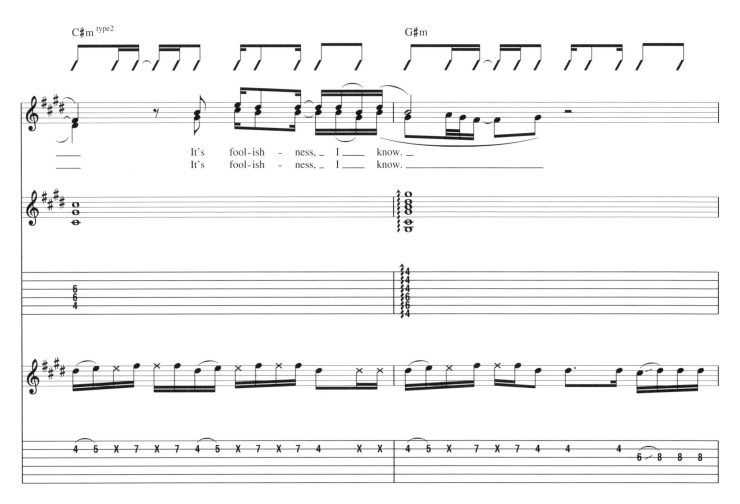

It's fool-ish - ness, __ I __ know. __
It's fool-ish - ness, __ I __ know. __

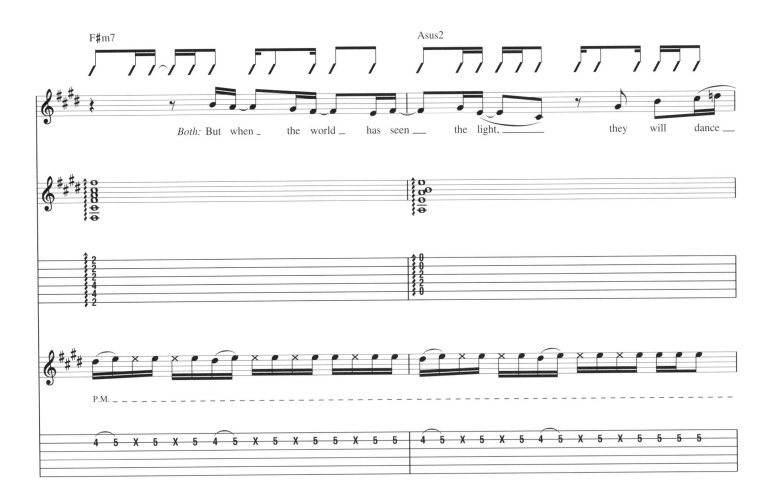

Both: But when __ the world __ has seen __ the light, ____ they will dance __

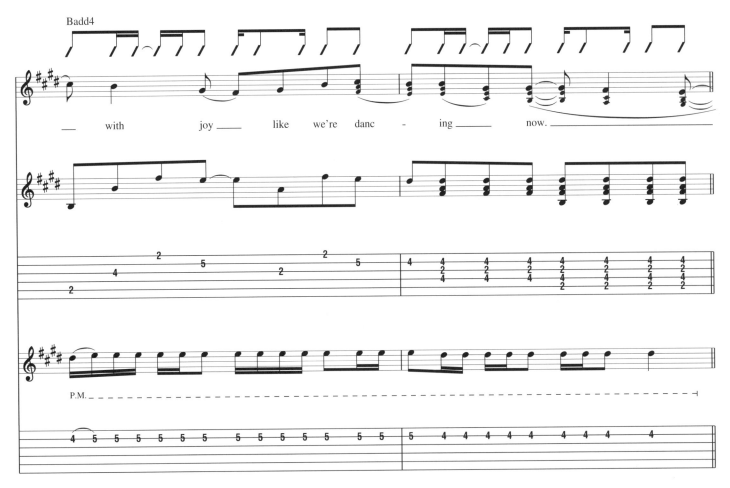

__ with joy ____ like we're danc - ing ____ now.

Outro-Chorus

Male: Oo, _____ I _____ can

I could sing of your love _____ for - ev - er.

sing. _____

Male: I lift the hands _ and praise _ the ho - ly name. _
Female: I lift the hands _ and praise _ the ho - ly name. _

I could sing of your love _____ for - ev - er.

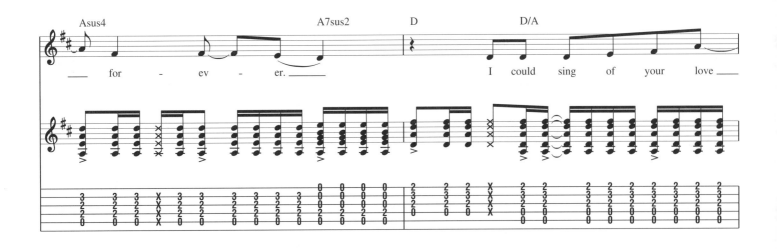

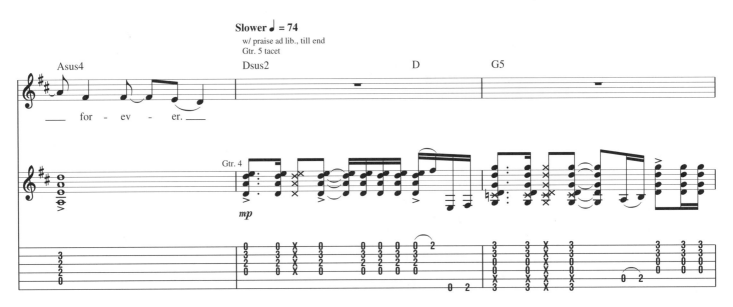

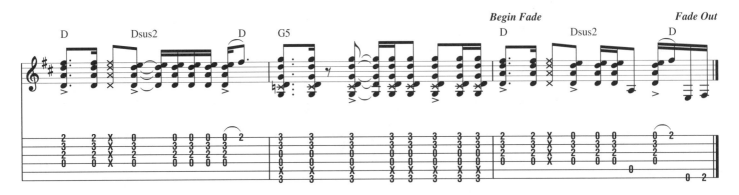

If We Are the Body

Words and Music by Mark Hall

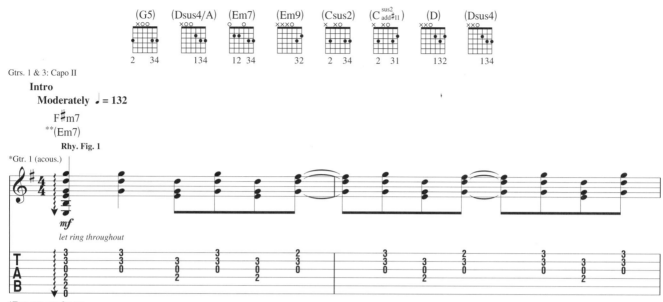

Gtrs. 1 & 3: Capo II

Intro
Moderately ♩ = 132

*Gtr. 1 (acous.)

let ring throughout

*Two gtrs. arr. for one.

**Symbols in parentheses represent chord names respective to capoed guitar.
Symbols above reflect actual sounding chords. Capoed fret is "0" in tab.
Chord symbols reflect basic harmony.

Gtr. 1: w/ Rhy. Fig. 1 (last 2 meas., 2 times)

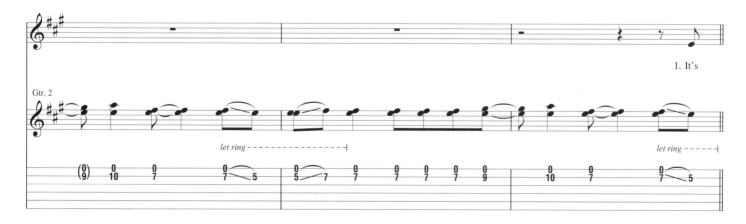

***Vol. swell

Verse

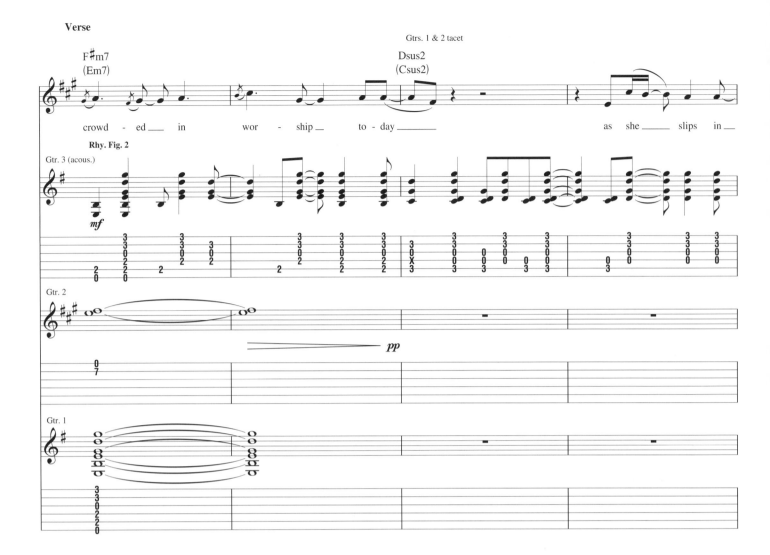

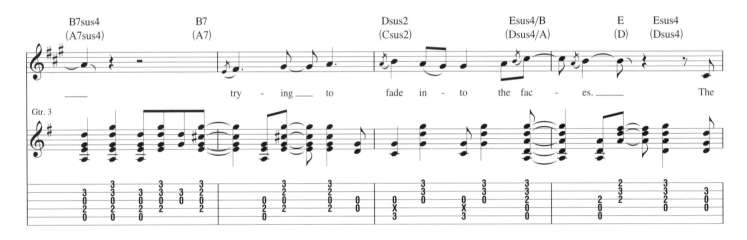

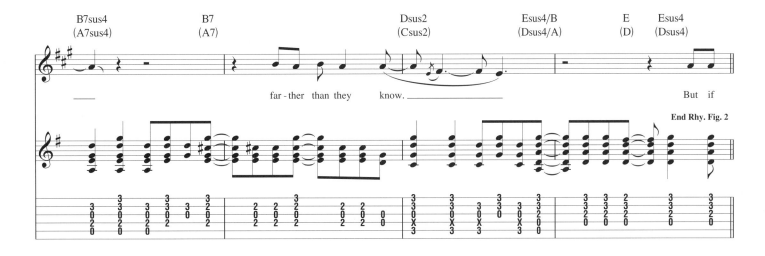

Chorus

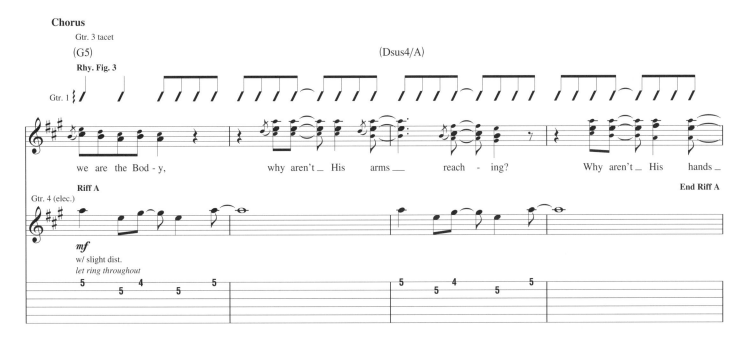

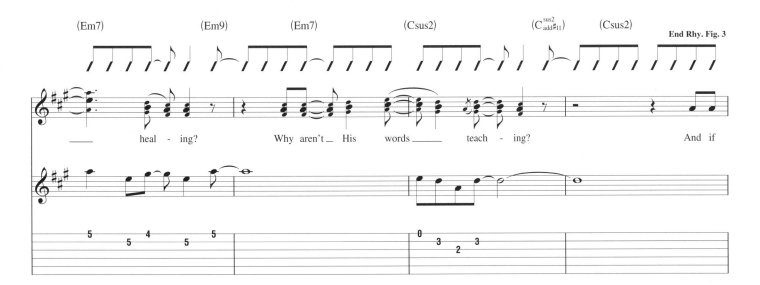

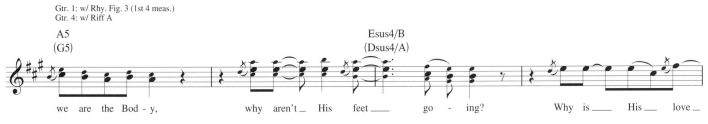

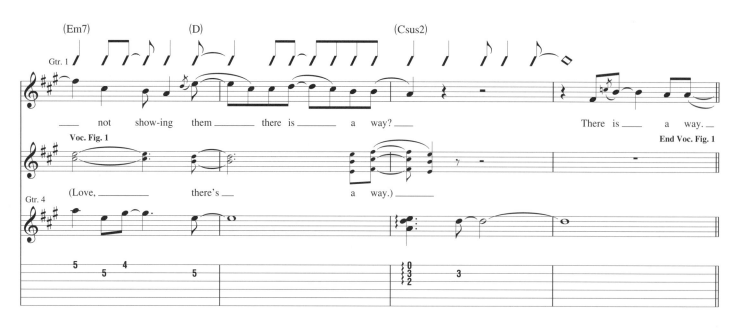

(Em7)   (D)   (Csus2)

Gtr. 1

____ not show-ing them ____ there is ____ a way? ____   There is ____ a way.

Voc. Fig. 1

End Voc. Fig. 1

(Love, ____ there's ____ a way.)

Gtr. 4

Interlude

Gtr. 1: w/ Rhy. Fig. 1
Gtr. 4 tacet

F#m7
(Em7)

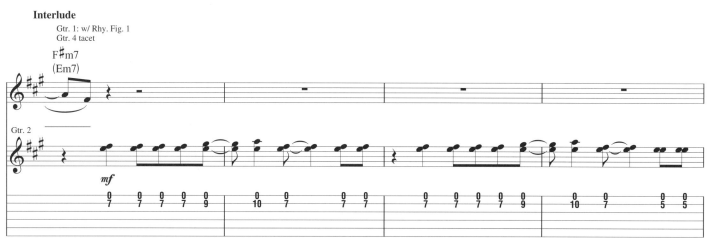

Gtr. 2

mf

Gtr. 1: w/ Rhy. Fig. 1 (last 2 meas., 2 times)

2. A

let ring

let ring

Verse

Gtr. 3: w/ Rhy. Fig. 2   Gtr. 2 tacet

F#m7   Dsus2
(Em7)   (Csus2)

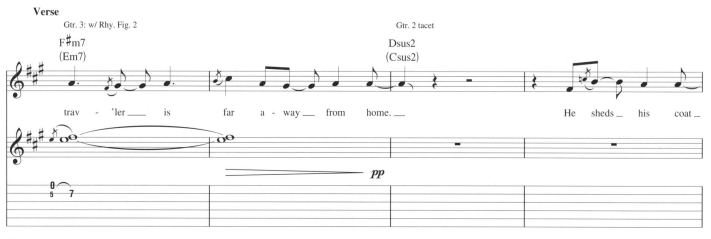

trav - 'ler ____ is   far a - way ____ from home.   He sheds ___ his coat ___

pp

Bridge

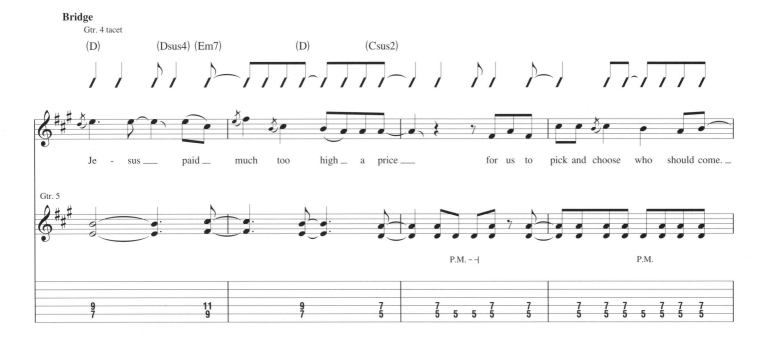

Je - sus __ paid __ much too high __ a price __ for us to pick and choose who should come. __

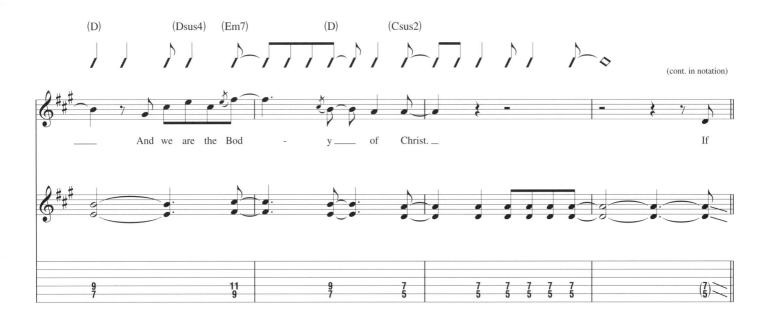

__ And we are the Bod - y __ of Christ. __ If

(cont. in notation)

Chorus

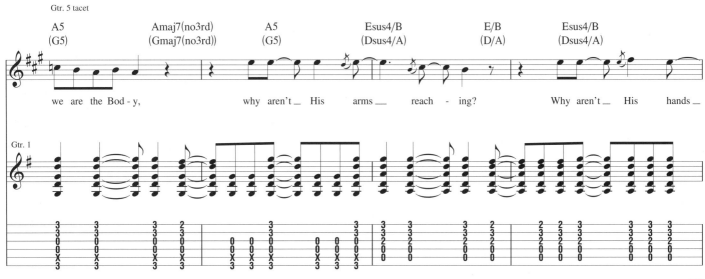

we are the Bod - y, why aren't __ His arms __ reach - ing? Why aren't __ His hands __

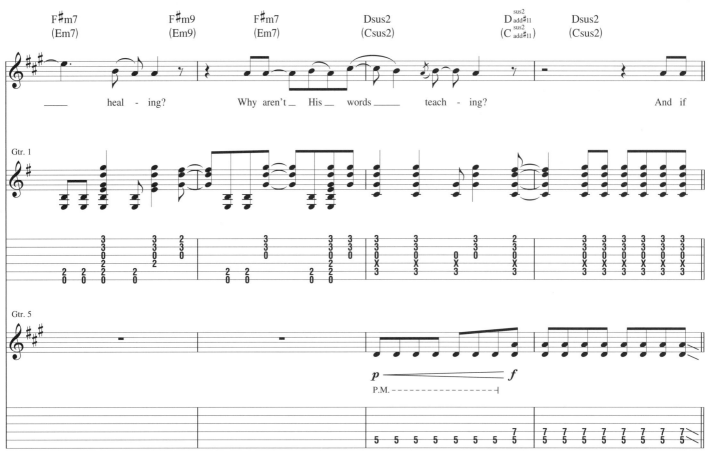

D.S.S. al Coda 2

Coda 1

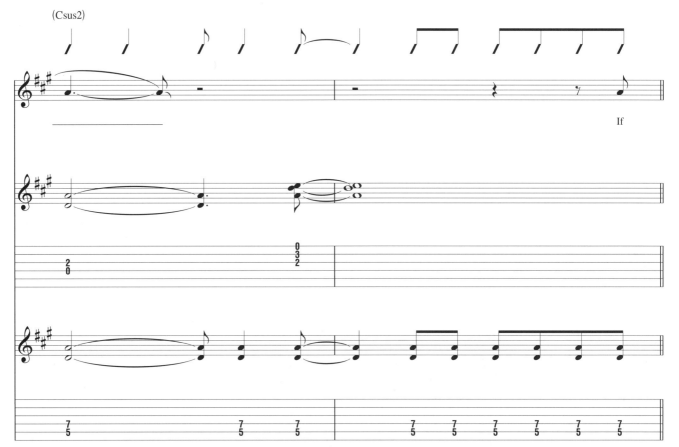

(Csus2)

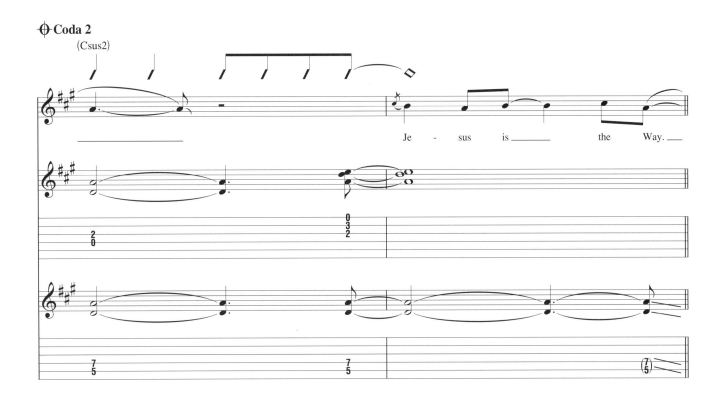

Je- sus is ____ the Way. ____

Outro

Gtr. 1: w/ Rhy. Fig. 1
Gtrs. 4 & 5 tacet

F#m7
(Em7)

You are ____ the One. ____

Gtr. 2

mf

let ring - - - - - - - - - -|

let ring - - -

F#m
(Em)

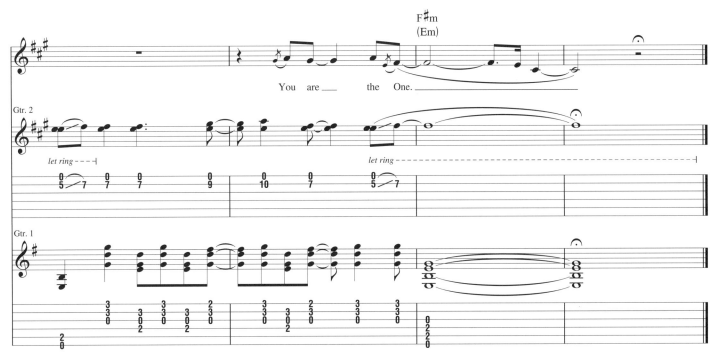

You are ____ the One. ____

Gtr. 2

let ring - - -|

let ring - - - - - - - - - - - - - - - - -|

Gtr. 1

Let Everything Else Go

Words and Music by Phil Keaggy

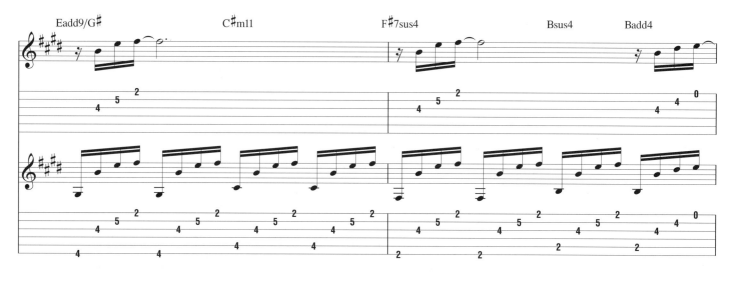

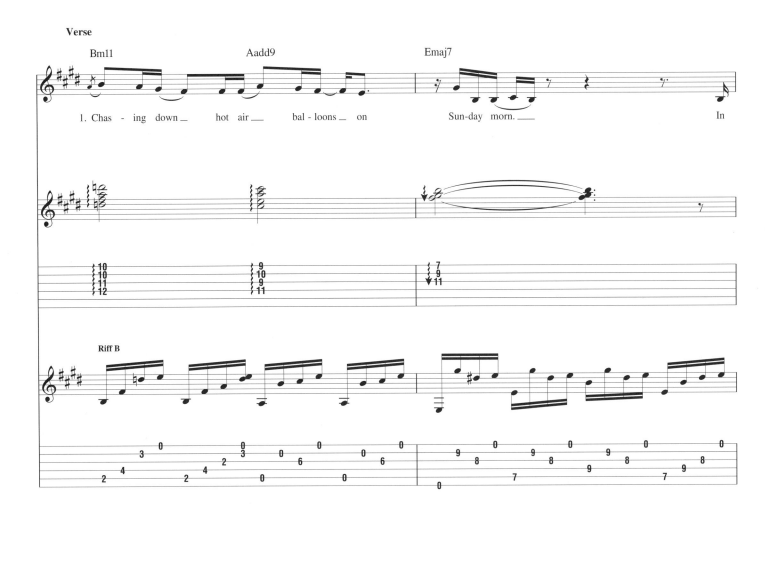

1. Chas - ing down ___ hot air ___ bal - loons ___ on Sun-day morn. ___ In

pace with a ___ fa - mil - iar tune, I reach for noth-ing less, ___ but ___ some-thing more. ___

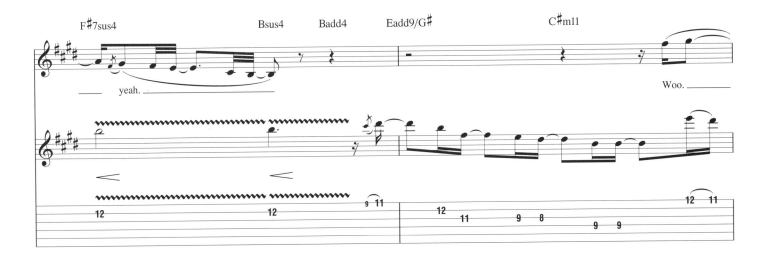

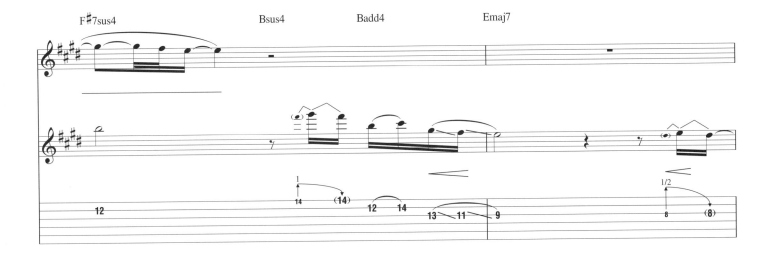

Verse

Gtrs. 1 & 2: w/ Riff B

2. Hold - in' con - ver - sa - tion with _____ a Friend _

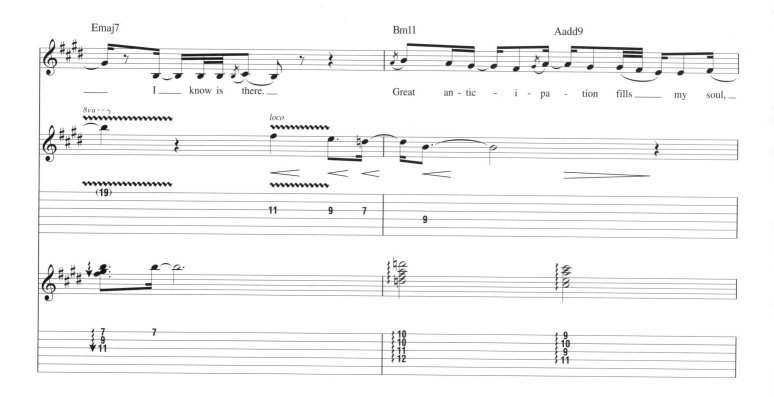

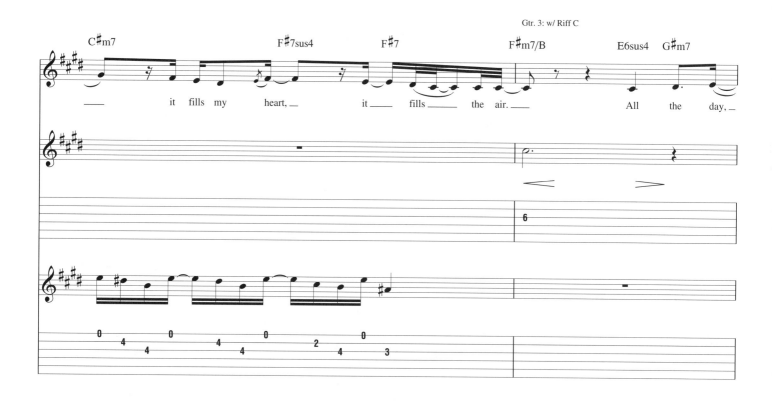

𝄉 Chorus

Gtr. 4 tacet
2nd time, Gtr. 3 tacet

*Composite arrangement

Interlude

Gtrs. 1 & 2: w/ Riff A
Gtr. 3: w/ Riff A1

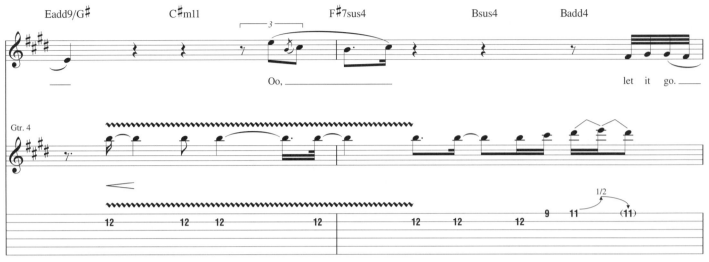

Guitar Solo

Gtrs. 1 & 2: w/ Riff B

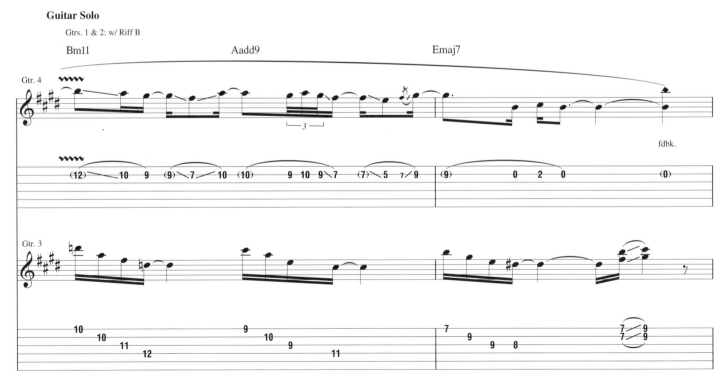

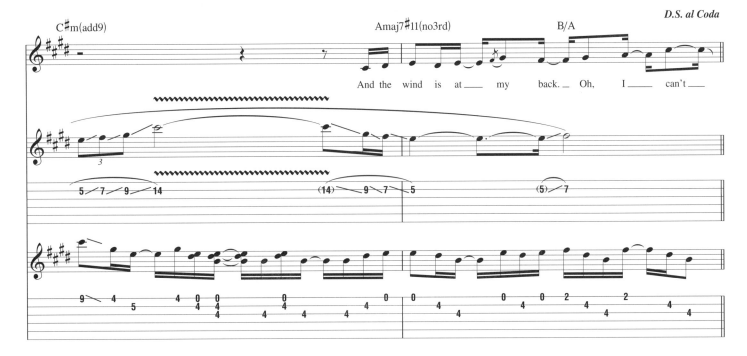

D.S. al Coda

And the wind is at ___ my back. Oh, I ___ can't

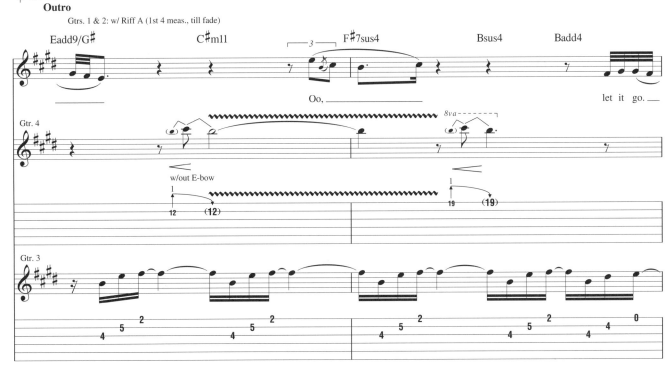

⊕ **Coda**
Outro

Gtrs. 1 & 2: w/ Riff A (1st 4 meas., till fade)

Oo, ___

let it go. ___

Gtr. 4

w/out E-bow

Gtr. 3

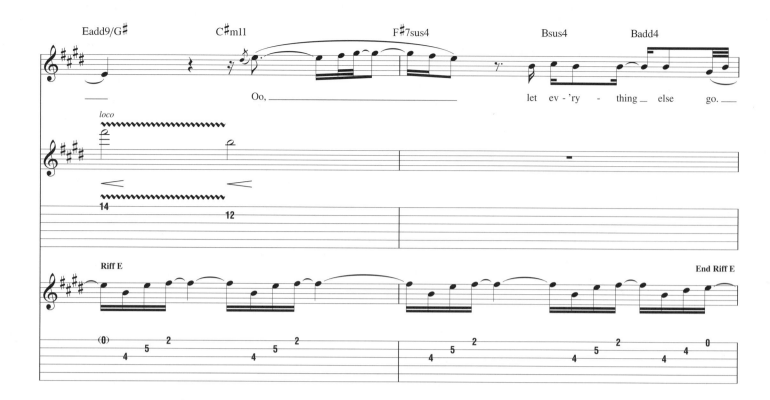

Oo, _____ let ev·'ry - thing __ else go.

Gtr. 3: w/ Riff E (till fade)

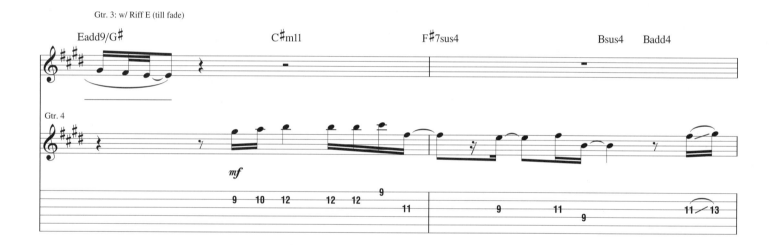

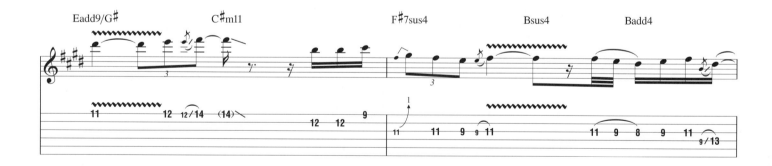

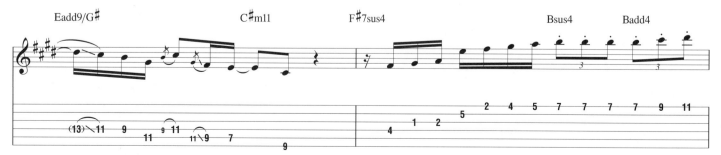

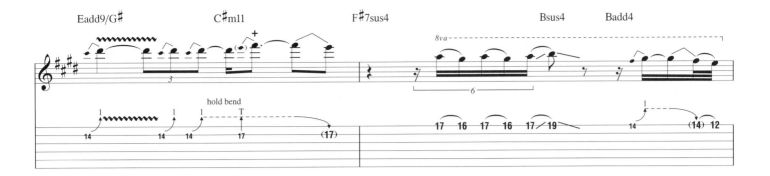

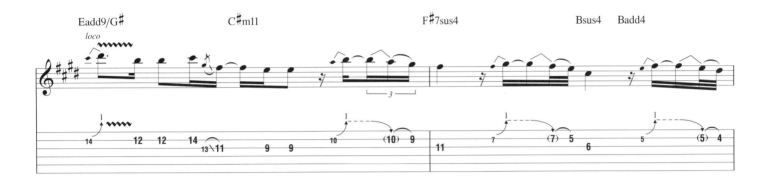

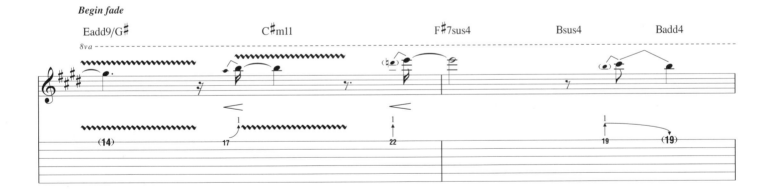

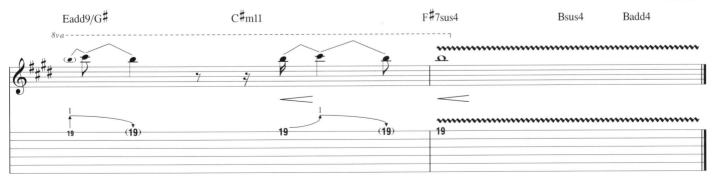

Listen to Our Hearts

Words and Music by Geoff Moore and Steven Curtis Chapman

Tune down 1/2 step:
(low to high) E♭-A♭-D♭-G♭-B♭-E♭

Intro

Moderately slow ♩ = 92

*Chord symbols reflect basic harmony.

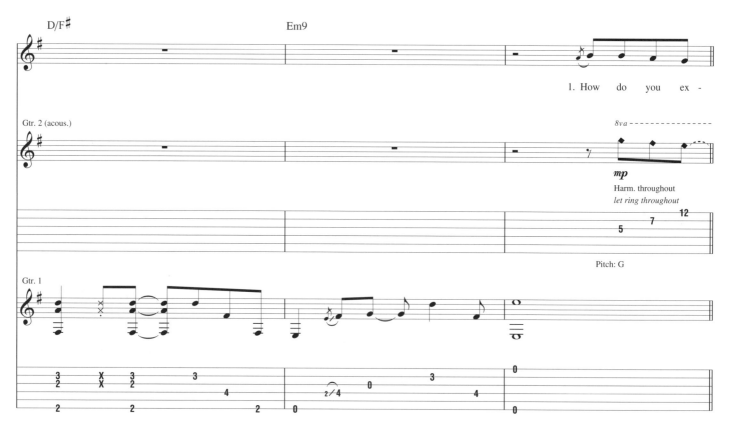

Verse

plain,   how do you de - scribe _   a   love that goes from

east   to   west _   and runs as deep as it is wide?   You know all our

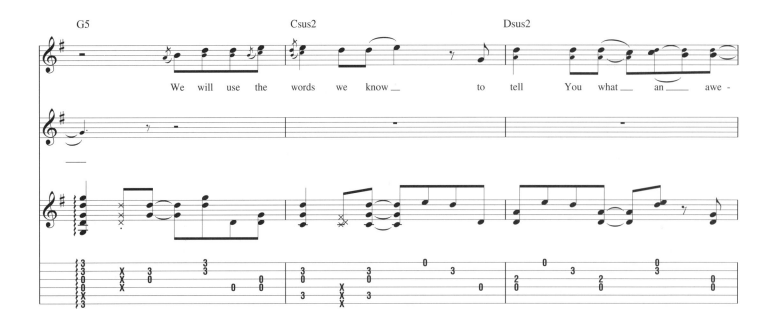

We will use the words we know ___ to tell You what ___ an ___ awe-

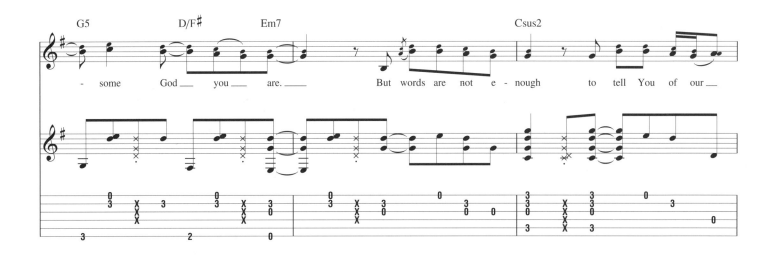

-some God ___ you ___ are. ___ But words are not e- nough to tell You of our ___

To Coda 1 ⊕
To Coda 2 ⊕

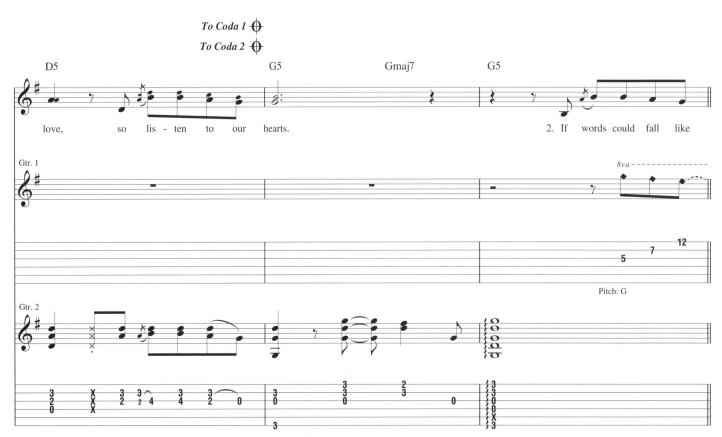

love, so lis - ten to our hearts. 2. If words could fall like

Piano Solo

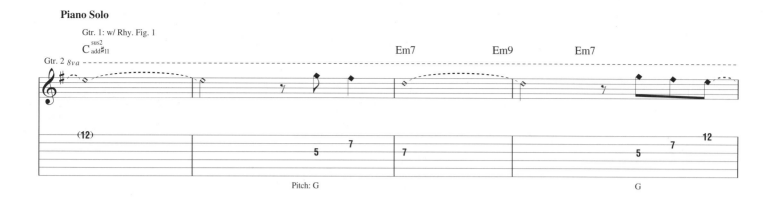

D.S.S. al Coda 2

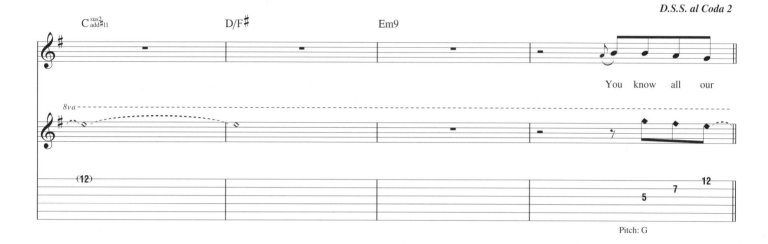

You know all our

Coda 2

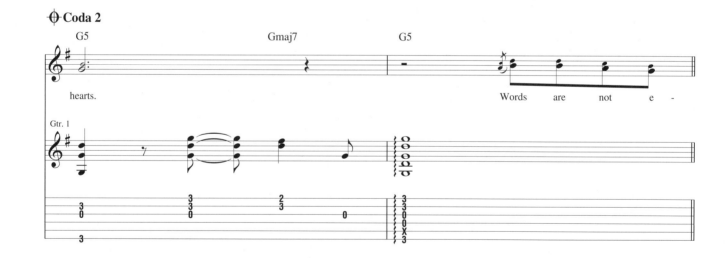

hearts.

Words are not e-

Outro

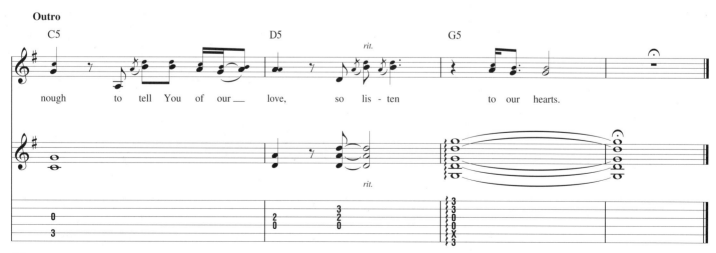

nough to tell You of our ___ love, so lis- ten to our hearts.

84

Mountain of God

Words and Music by Mac Powell and Brown Bannister

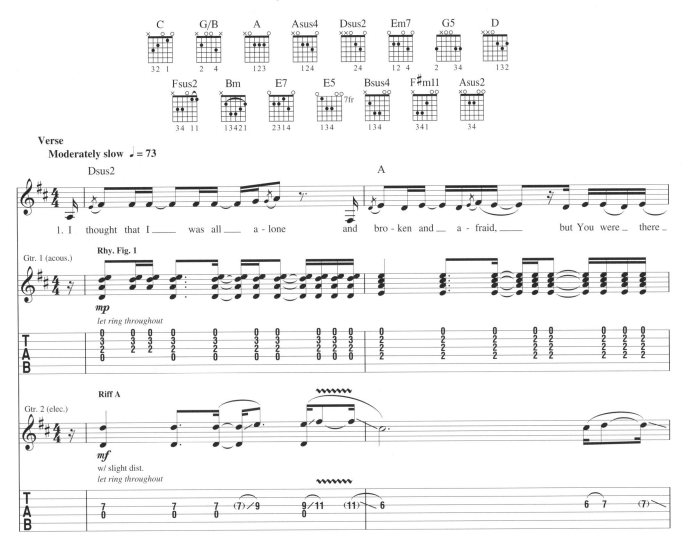

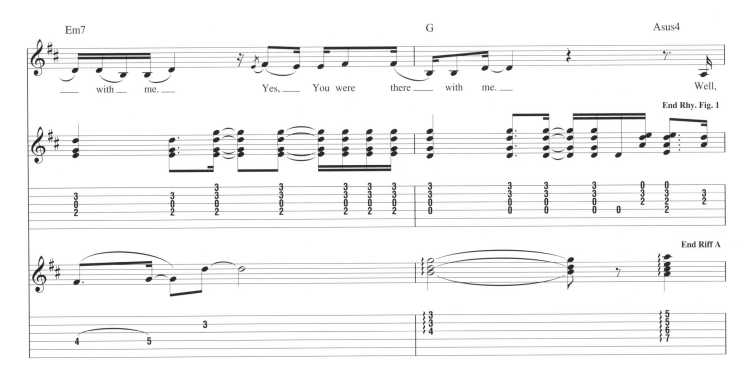

and I did-n't e-ven know ___ that I had lost ___ my way, ___ but You were ___ there ___

___ with ___ me. ___ Yes, You were there ___ with ___ me. ___ Un - til You

Pre-Chorus

o - pened up ___ my eyes ___ I nev - er knew _____ that I

could - n't ev - er make ___ it with - out You. ___ And e - ven though the

Chorus

*Composite arrangement

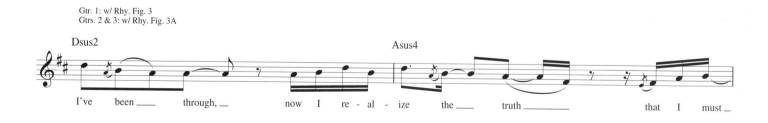

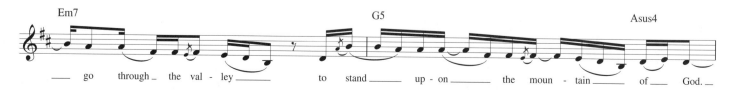

Verse

Gtr. 1: w/ Rhy. Fig. 1 (2 times)
Gtr. 2: w/ Riff A (2 times)

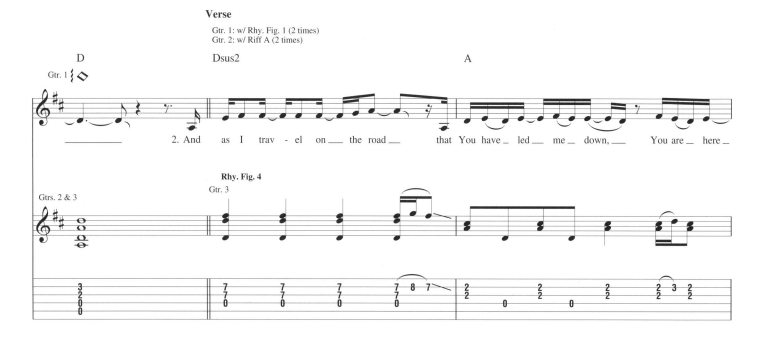

2. And as I trav-el on the road that You have led me down, You are here

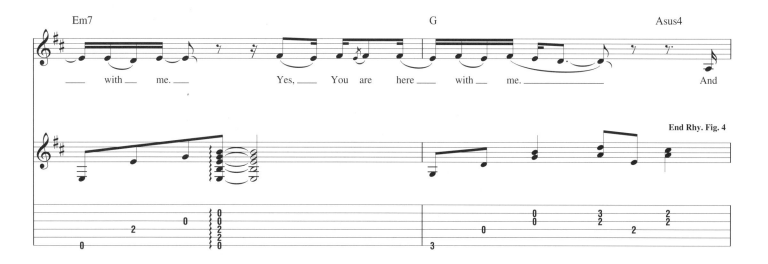

with me. Yes, You are here with me. And

Gtr. 3: w/ Rhy. Fig. 4

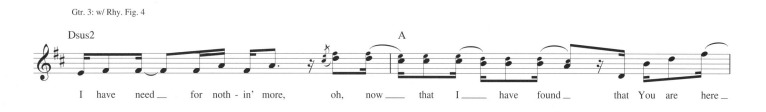

I have need for noth-in' more, oh, now that I have found that You are here

with me. Yes, You are here with me. Well, I con-

(Yeah.)

Pre-Chorus

Gtr. 1: w/ Rhy. Fig. 2
Gtr. 3: w/ Riff B

fess from time __ to time __ I lose __ my way, _____ but You were

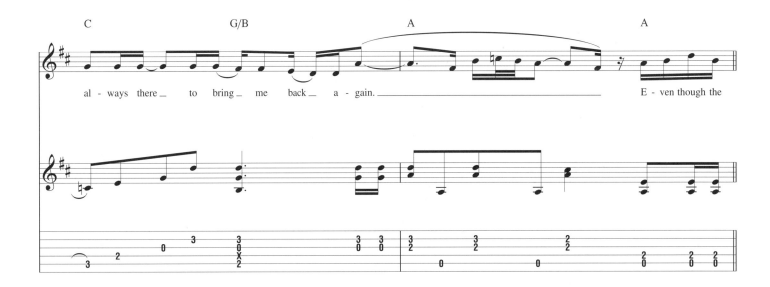

al - ways there __ to bring __ me back __ a - gain. _____ E - ven though the

Chorus

Gtr. 1: w/ Rhy. Fig. 3 (2 times)

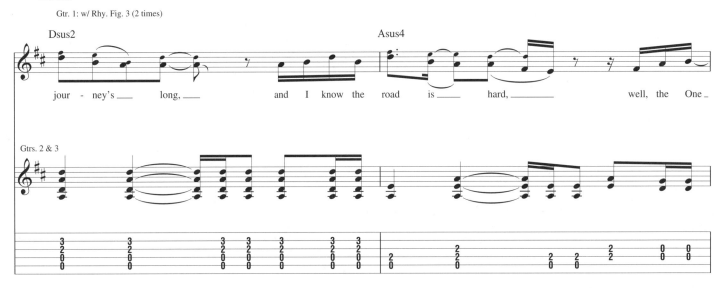

jour - ney's __ long, __ and I know the road is __ hard, _____ well, the One __

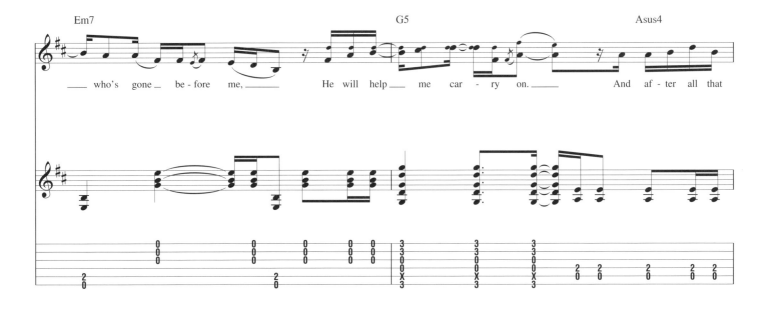

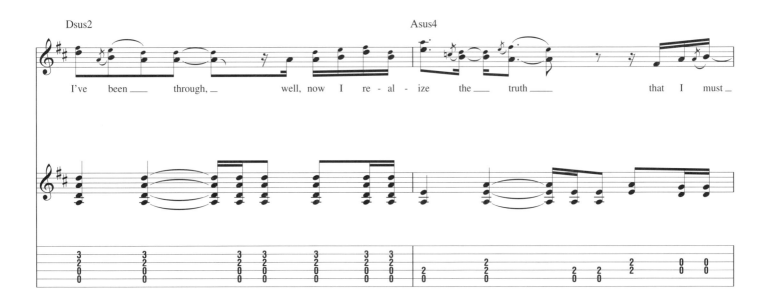

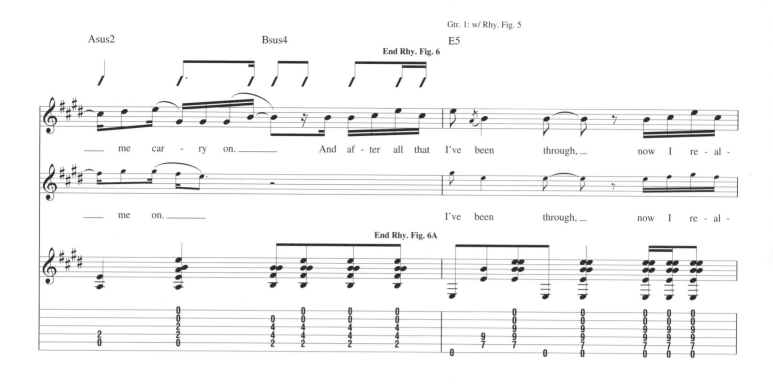

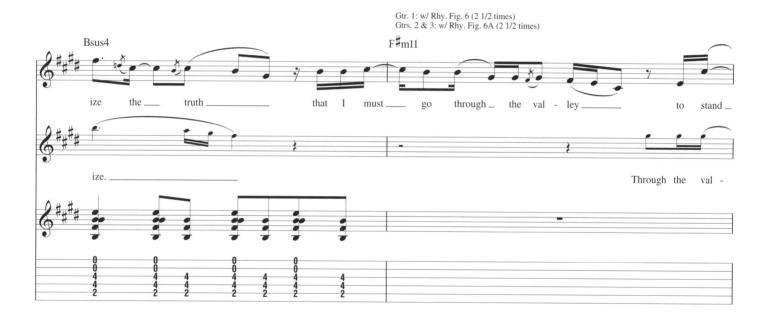

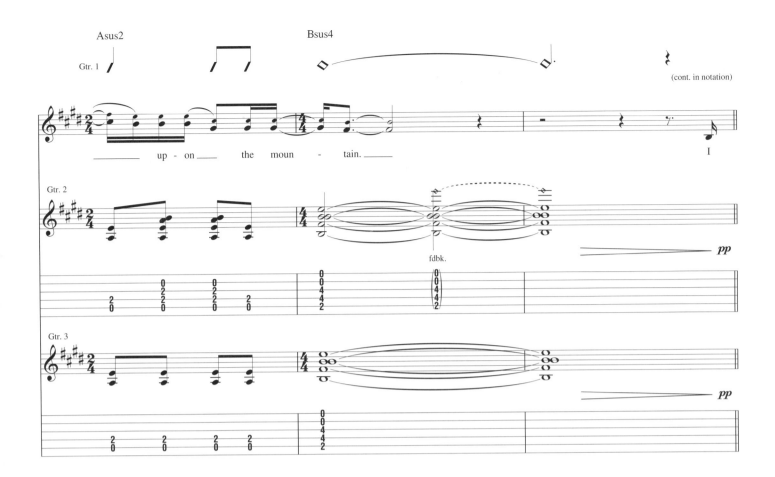

up - on ___ the moun - tain. ___

I

(cont. in notation)

Outro

Gtrs. 2 & 3 tacet

E5   Bsus4

thought that I ___ was all ___ a - lone, ___   bro - ken and ___ a - fraid, ___   but You are ___ here ___

Gtr. 1

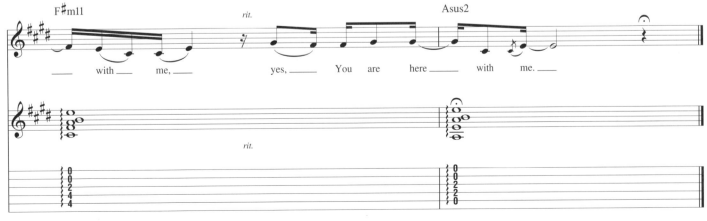

F#m11   *rit.*   Asus2

___ with ___ me, ___   yes, ___ You are here ___ with ___ me.

My Will

Words and Music by Toby McKeehan, Michael Tait, Joey Elwood and Daniel Pitts

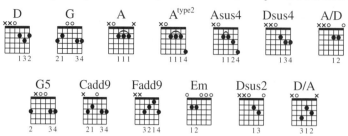

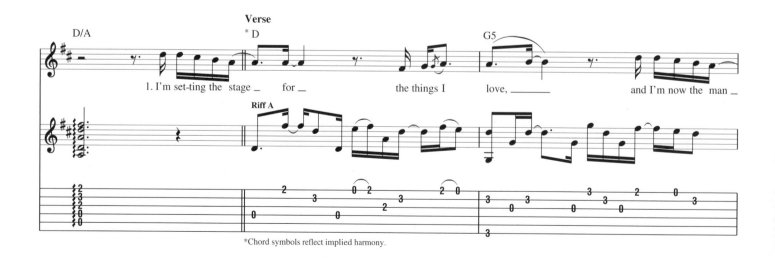

*Chord symbols reflect implied harmony.

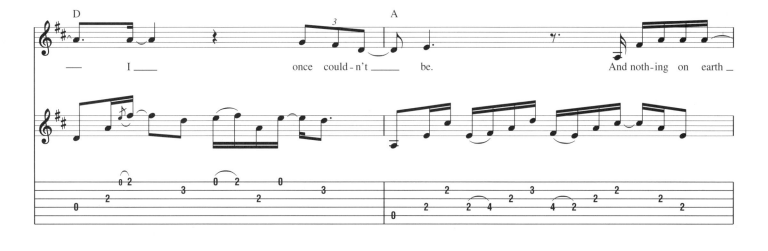

I ___ once could-n't ___ be. And noth-ing on earth ___

___ could ___ now ev-er move ___ me. I now have the will ___ and ___ the strength a

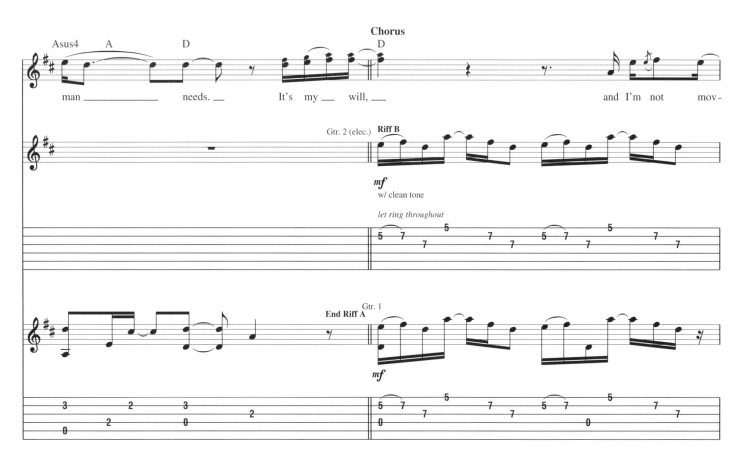

man ___ needs. ___ It's my ___ will, ___ and I'm not mov-

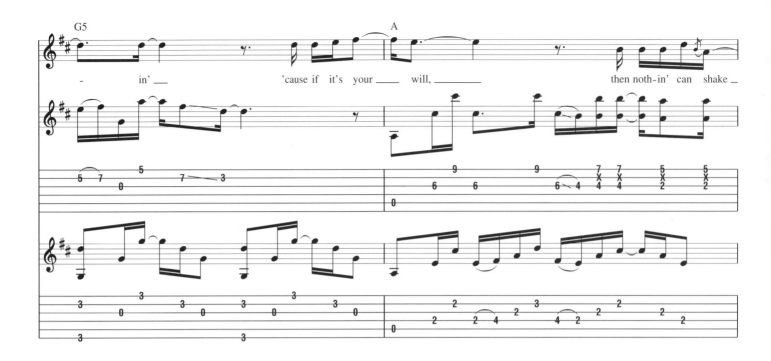

-in' ___ 'cause if it's your ___ will, _____ then noth-in' can shake ___

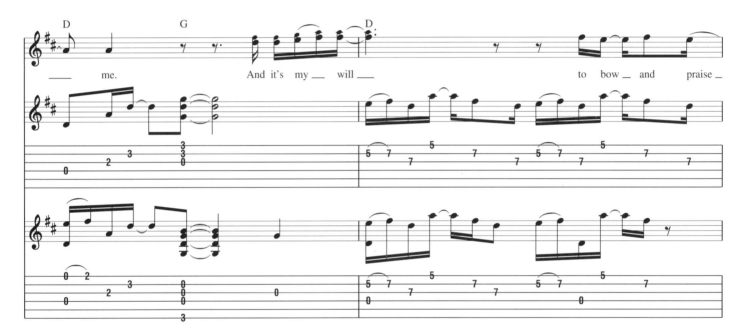

___ me. And it's my ___ will ___ to bow ___ and praise ___

___ you. ___ I now have the will to praise ___ my

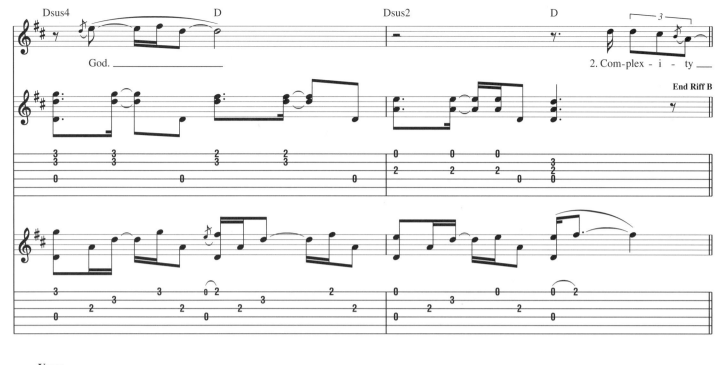

God. _____

2. Com-plex-i-ty _____

End Riff B

Verse

Gtr. 1: w/ Riff A

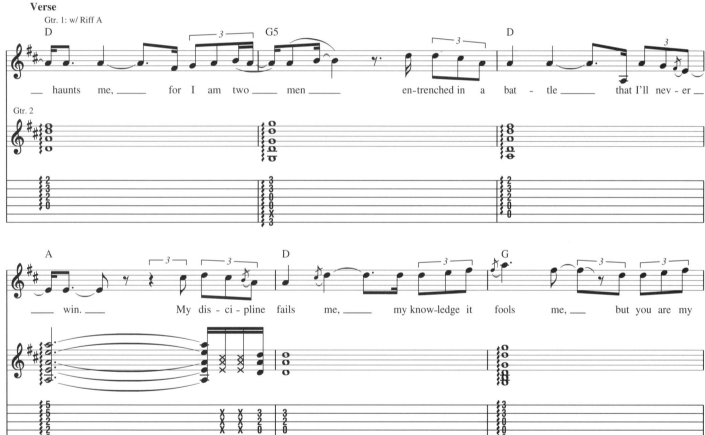

___ haunts me, _____ for I am two ___ men _____ en-trenched in a bat - tle _____ that I'll nev - er ___ win. ___ My dis - ci - pline fails me, _____ my know-ledge it fools me, ___ but you are my

Gtr. 2

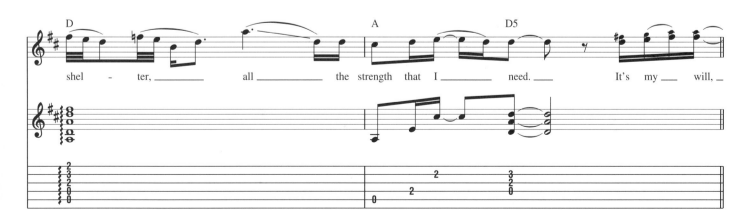

shel - ter, _____ all _____ the strength that I _____ need. ____ It's my ___ will, __

% **Chorus**

Gtr. 2: w/ Riff B

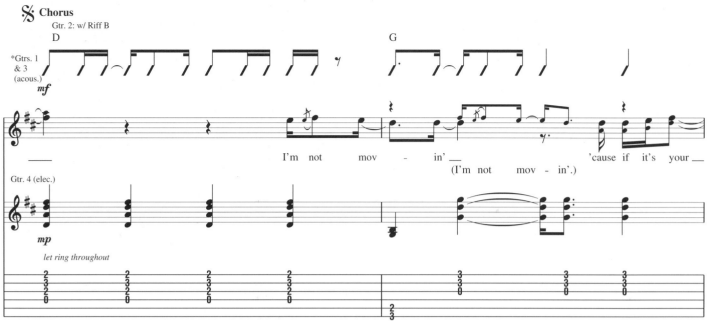

*Gtrs. 1 & 3 (acous.)

mf

Gtr. 4 (elec.)

mp

let ring throughout

I'm not mov - in' ___ 'cause if it's your ___
(I'm not mov - in'.)

*Composite arrangement.

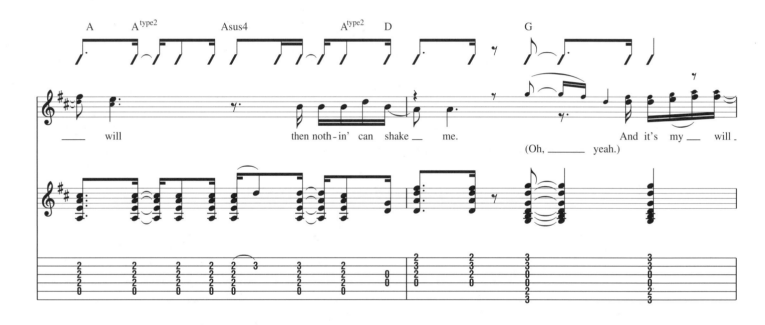

___ will then noth-in' can shake ___ me. And it's my ___ will ___
(Oh, ___ yeah.)

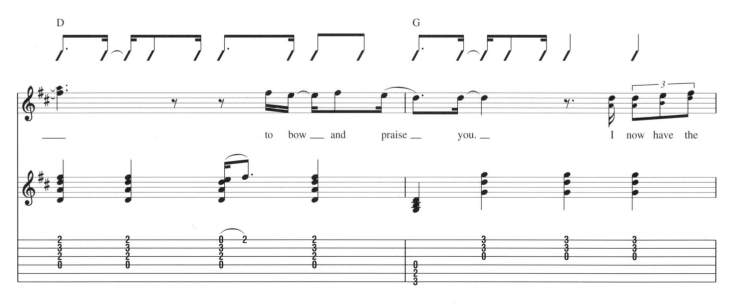

___ to bow ___ and praise ___ you. ___ I now have the

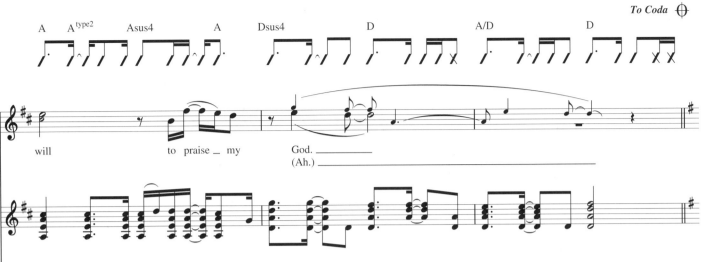

Interlude

3. I'm learn-in' to give _

Verse

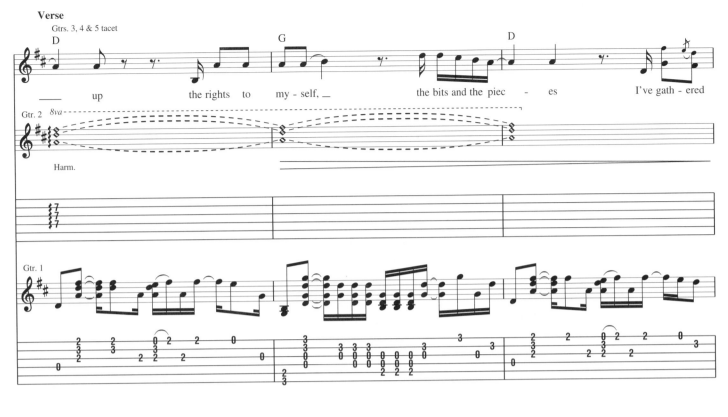

____ up the rights to my-self, ____ the bits and the piec - es I've gath - ered

as wealth. ____ It nev - er com - pared ____ to the joy that you ____

D.S. al Coda

____ bring ____ me. The peace that you show ____ me _____ is the strength that I ____ need. It's my ____ will ____

*Composite arrangement.

will   then noth-ing can shake __ me. _____ And it's my __ will __

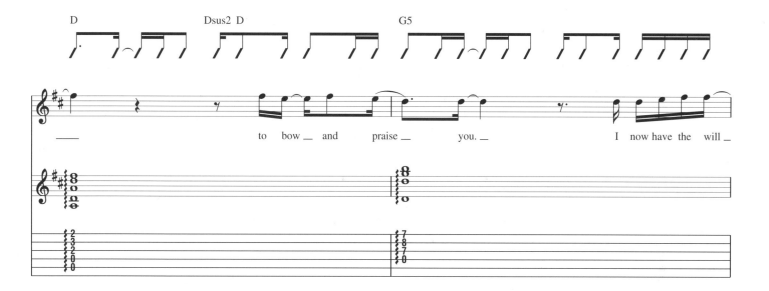

__   to bow __ and praise __ you. __   I now have the will __

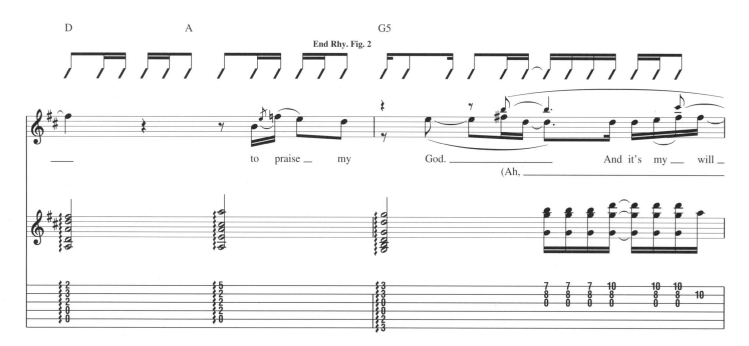

__   to praise __ my   God. _____ And it's my __ will _____

(Ah, _____

One of These Days

Words and Music by Jeromy Deibler

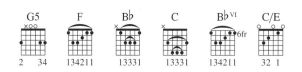

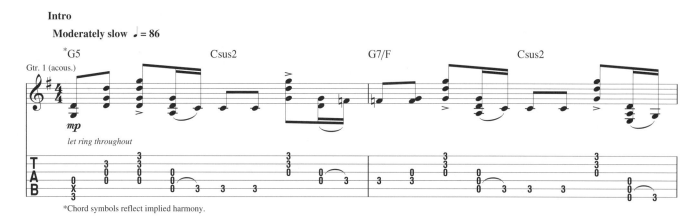

Intro

Moderately slow ♩ = 86

*Chord symbols reflect implied harmony.

let ring throughout

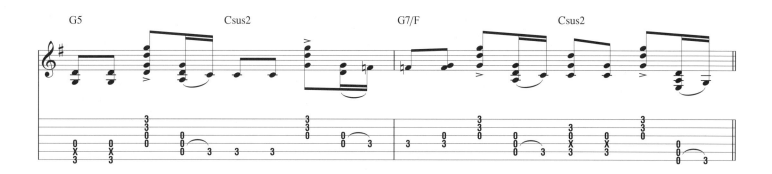

Verse

3rd time, Gtr. 2 tacet

1. One of these days I'm gon-na fly _____ o-ver the moun-tain. _____
2. One of these days I'm gon-na do _____ all the things that I've nev-er done. _____
3. One of these days I'll fi-n'ly be _____ in a place where there's no more need, _____

Rhy. Fig. 1

Gtr. 1

One of these days I'm gon - na ride ___ on the sil - ver lin - ing. ___
I'm ___ gon - na fin - ish all ___ the rac - es that I've run, but I've nev - er won. ___
no more pain and no ___ more grief, ___ no more fool - ish dis - be - lief. ___

One of these days I'm gon - na wit - ness all I've been miss - ing. ___
And I'm gon - na see a mil - lion fac - es and rec - og - nize ev - 'ry one. ___
And all the joy ___ there will be ___ when at last we fi - n'ly see.

3rd time, Gtr. 2: w/ Fill 1

1.

G7/F   Csus2   G5   Csus2

End Rhy. Fig. 1

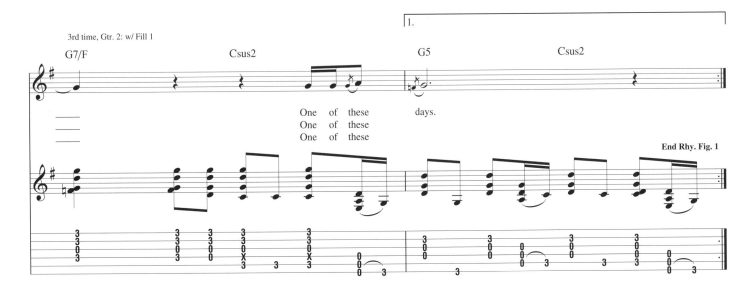

One of these days.
One of these
One of these

Fill 1
Gtr. 2

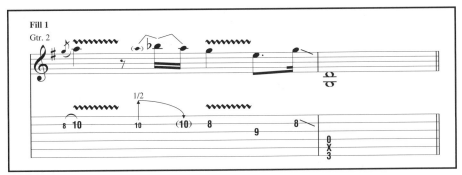

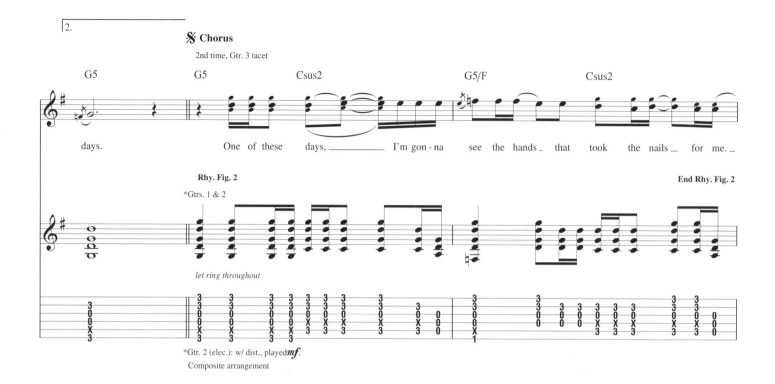

2.

%. **Chorus**

2nd time, Gtr. 3 tacet

days. One of these days, _____ I'm gon-na see the hands _ that took the nails _ for me. _

Rhy. Fig. 2

End Rhy. Fig. 2

*Gtrs. 1 & 2

let ring throughout

*Gtr. 2 (elec.): w/ dist., played **mf**.*
Composite arrangement

Gtrs. 1 & 2: w/ Rhy. Fig. 2 (2 times)

_____ One of these days, _____ I'm gon-na hold the key _ to the man-sion built for me. _

_____ One of these days, _____ I'm gon-na walk the streets _ of gold that were paved for me. _

_____ One of these _____ days, _____ I'm gon-na see my {1., 2. Sav - ior}
{3. Je - sus}

Gtrs. 1 & 2

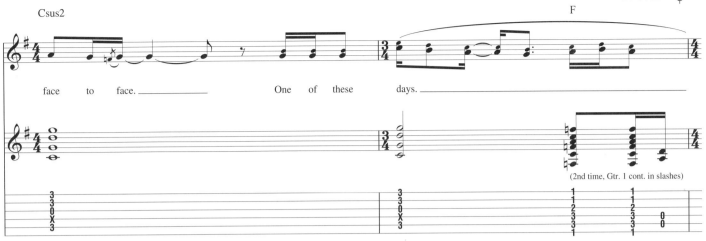

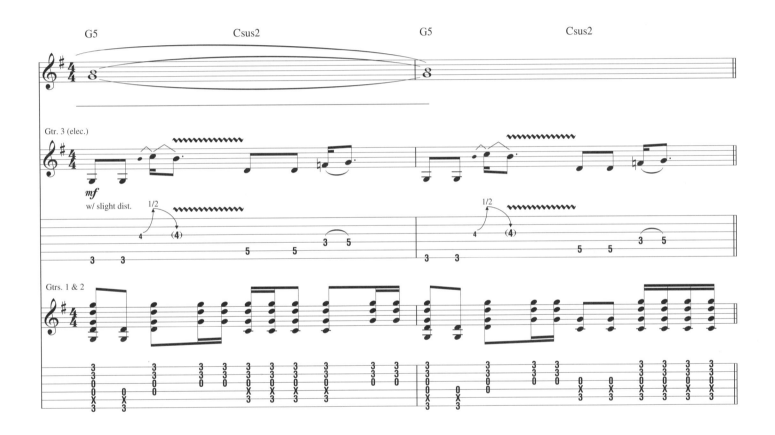

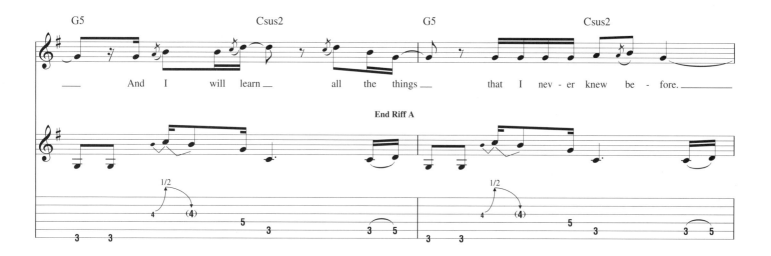

And I will learn ___ all the things ___ that I nev - er knew be - fore. ___

End Riff A

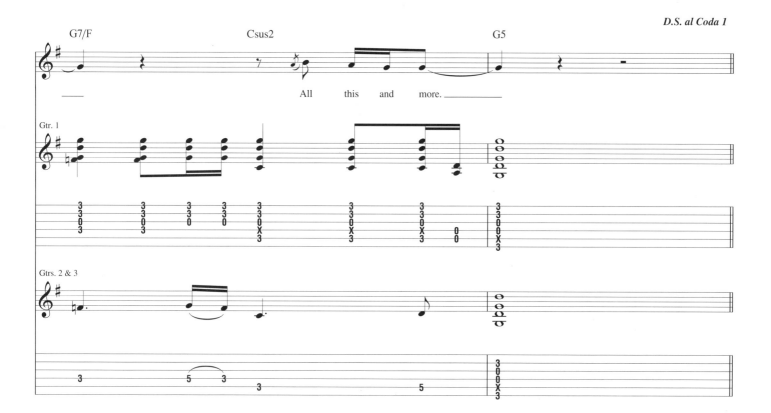

D.S. al Coda 1

All this and more. ___

Gtr. 1

Gtrs. 2 & 3

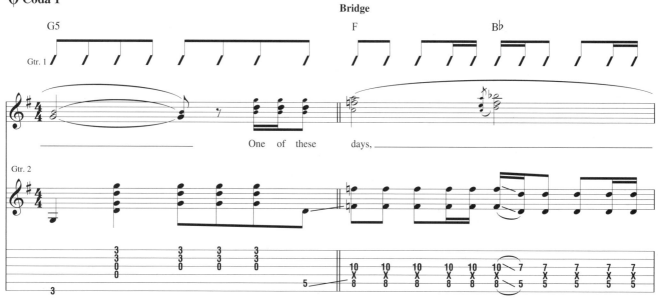

Coda 1

Bridge

Gtr. 1

One of these days, ___

Gtr. 2

one of these days.

One of these days,

*Bass plays E♭.   **Bass plays D.

one of these days.

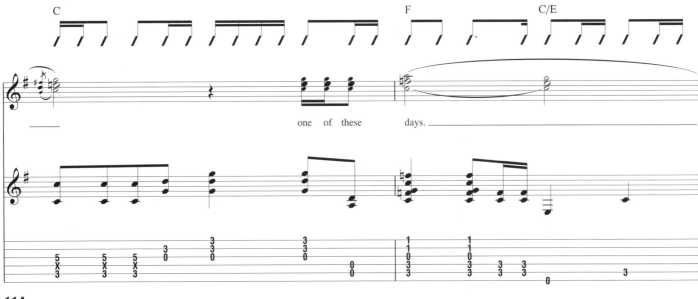

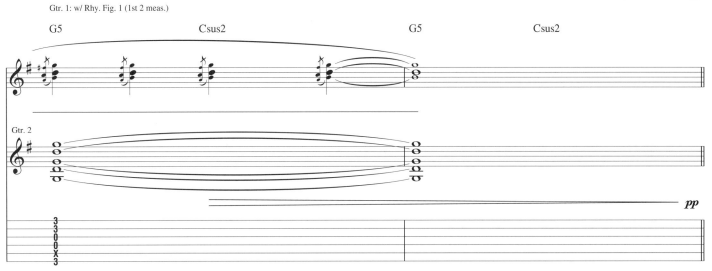

Gtr. 1: w/ Rhy. Fig. 1 (1st 2 meas.)

Coda 2

Gtr. 1: w/ Rhy. Fig. 1 (1st 3 meas.)
Gtr. 2: w/ Riff A

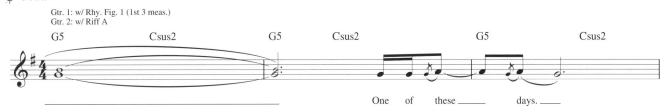

One of these days.

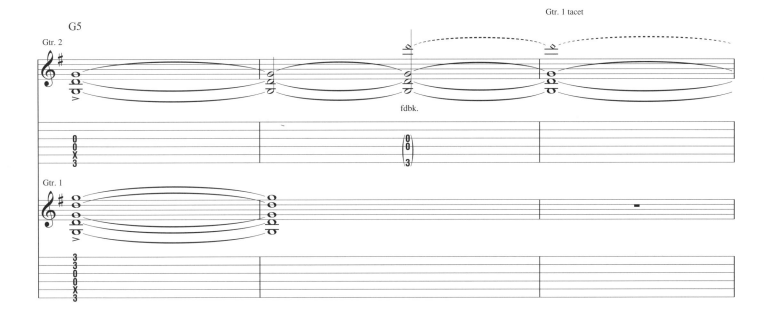

Gtr. 1 tacet

fdbk.

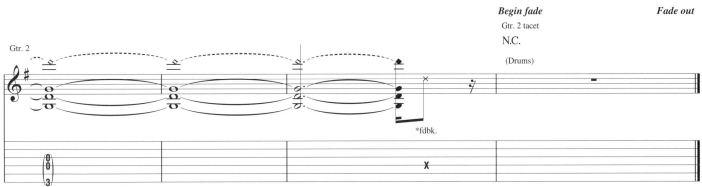

Begin fade

Fade out

Gtr. 2 tacet

N.C.

(Drums)

*fdbk.

*Microphonic fdbk., not caused by string vibration.

That Kind of Love

Words and Music by Gordon Kennedy and Jenny Yates

Intro
Moderately ♩ = 97

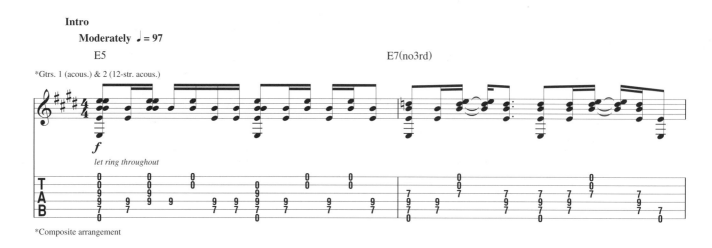

*Gtrs. 1 (acous.) & 2 (12-str. acous.)

*Composite arrangement

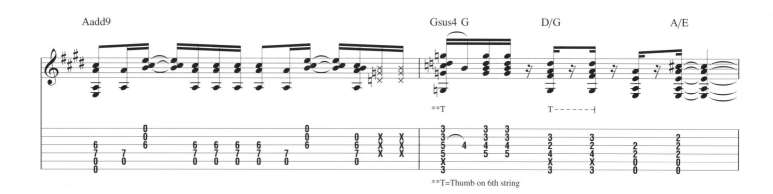

**T=Thumb on 6th string

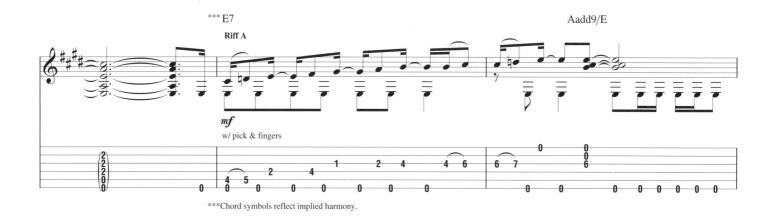

***Chord symbols reflect implied harmony.

Verse

Gtrs. 1 & 2: w/ Riff A (2 times)

1. Tell me the sto - ry a - bout the Man who came down from the sky, who healed the bro - ken heart - ed with His hand and dried the tear dimmed eye.

Pre-Chorus

Oh, I would give an - y - thing I would give
(Oh, I would give

Gtrs. 1 & 2

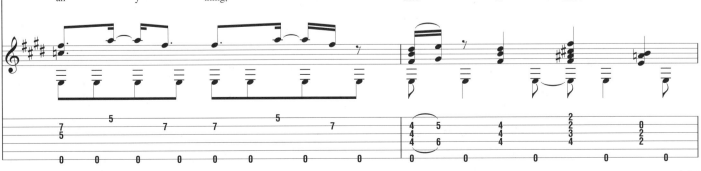

to see Him face to face. And,
an - y - thing, face to face.

⊕ Coda 1

Interlude

Chorus

Gtrs. 1 & 2: w/ Rhy. Fig. 1 (1st 3 meas.)

Oo, ___ I ___ wan - na find ___ that kind ___ of love. ___

D.S.S. al Coda 2

___ They say that it ___ runs in ___ His blood. ___

⊕ Coda 2

Outro

Undo Me

Words and Music by Jennifer Knapp

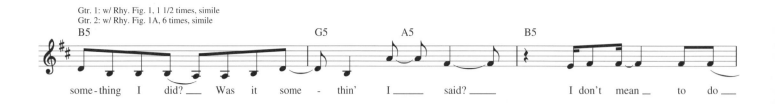

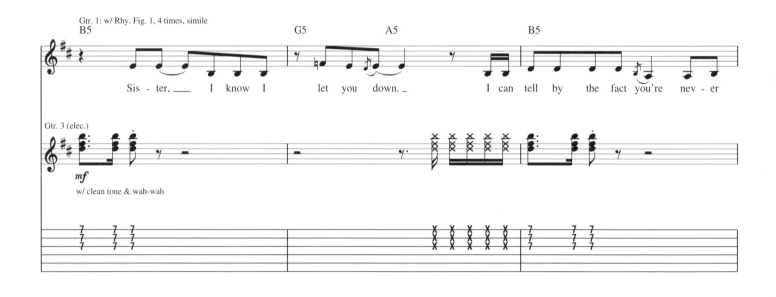

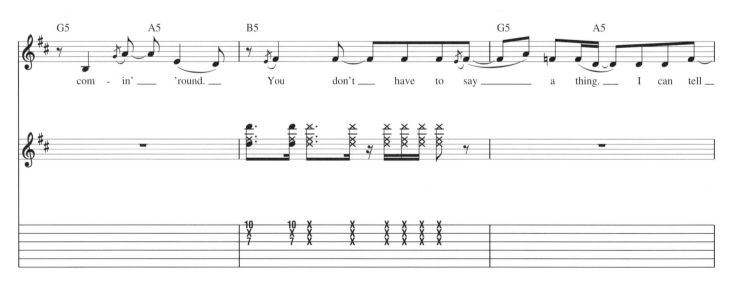

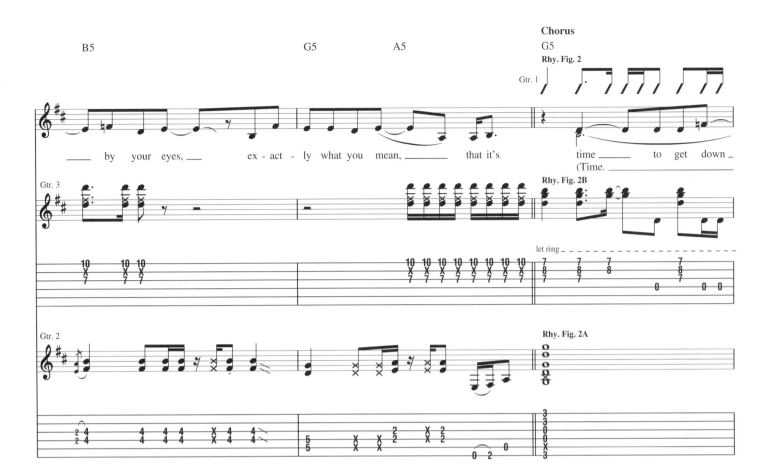

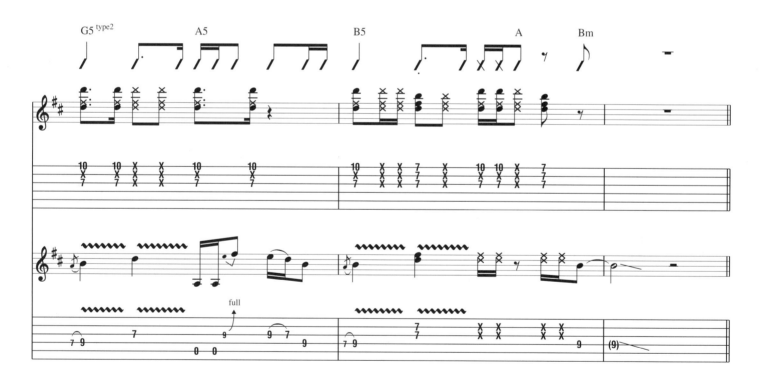

Verse

Gtr. 1: w/ Rhy. Fig. 1, 3 1/2 times, simile
Gtr. 2: w/ Rhy. Fig. 1A, 8 times, simile
Gtr. 3 tacet

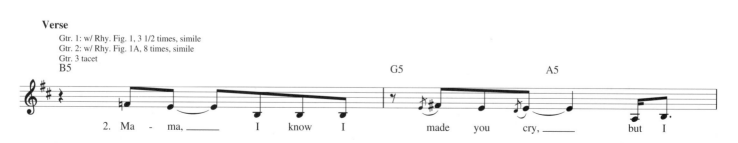

never meant to hurt you. I nev-er meant to ___ lie. ___ While the world ___ shook it's head ___

in shame, ___ I let you take the blame. ___

Gtr. 1: w/ Rhy. Fill 1

Gtr. 1: w/ Rhy. Fig. 1, 4 times, simile

Bro - ther, ___ I know you ___ lab - ered so ___ hard ___ to ___ please, ___ yeah, ___

Gtr. 3

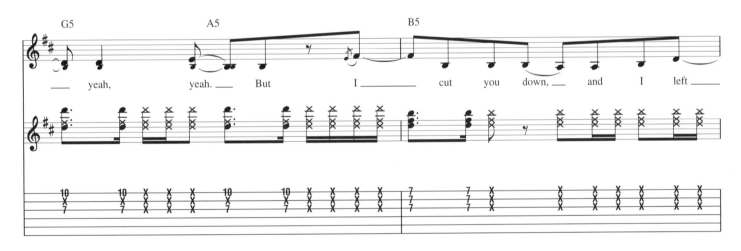

___ yeah, ___ yeah. ___ But I ___ cut you down, ___ and I left ___

___ you on your knees. ___ Well, I ___ know it must ___ be, yeah.

Outro

Gtr. 1: w/ Rhy. Fig. 1, 1 1/2 times, simile

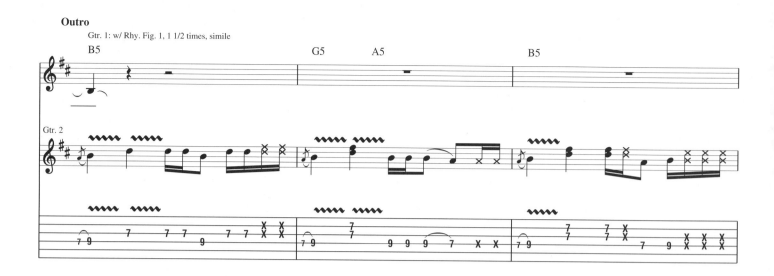

Gtr. 1: w/ Rhy. Fill 1

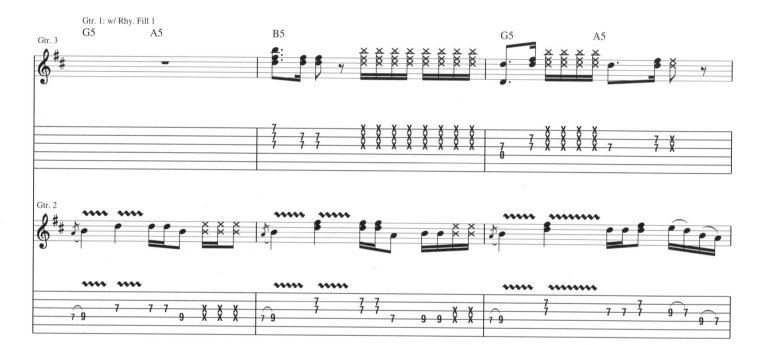

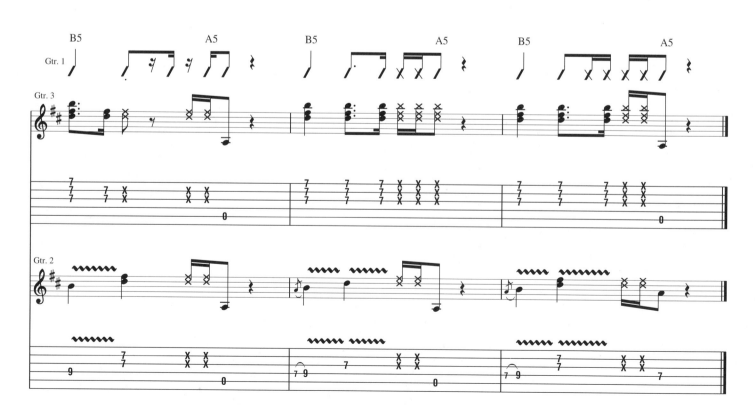

What If

Words and Music by Jadon Lavik, Adam Watts and Andy Dodd

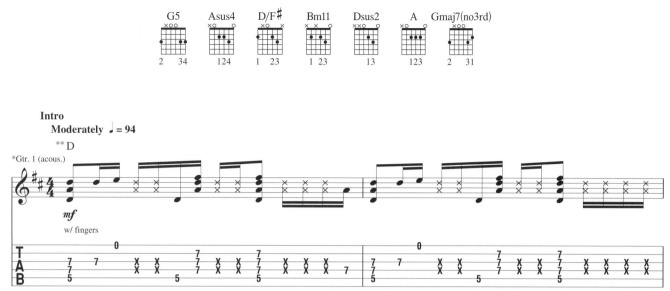

*Two gtrs. arr. for one.

**Chord symbols reflect basic harmony.

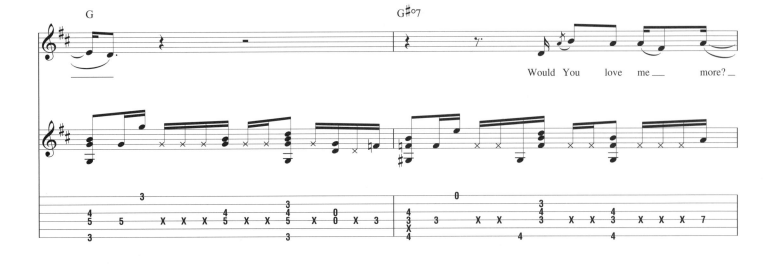

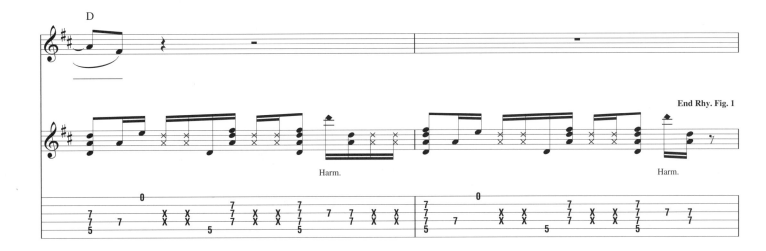

Gtr. 1: w/ Rhy. Fig. 1

What if I were ev-'ry-one's first choice? ___ What if I went far-ther than be-fore?

What if I stood high a-bove the rest, ___ then would You love me ___ more? ___

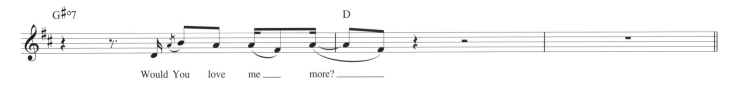

Would You love me ___ more? ___

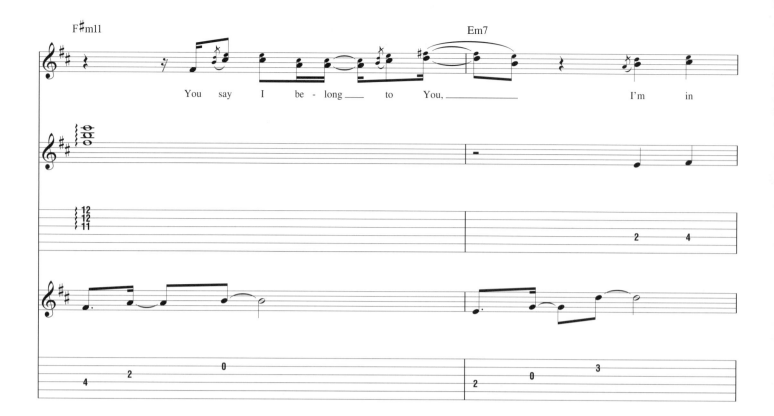

You say I be - long ____ to You, ____ I'm in

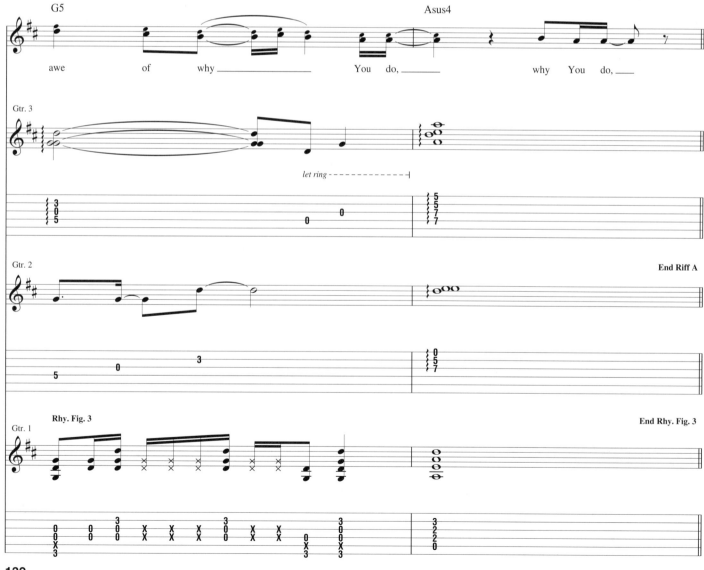

awe of why ____ You do, ____ why You do, ____

Gtr. 3

let ring - - - - - - - - - - - -

Gtr. 2

End Riff A

Rhy. Fig. 3

Gtr. 1

End Rhy. Fig. 3

Interlude

Gtr. 1: w/ Rhy. Fig. 1 (1st 4 meas.)
Gtr. 3 tacet

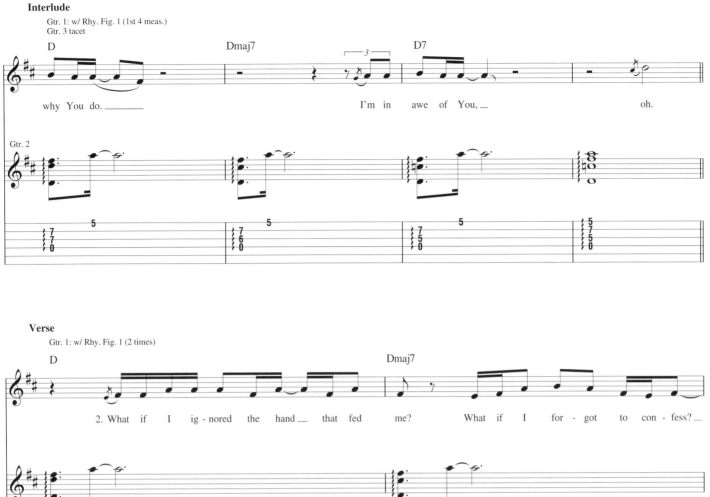

why You do. _____   I'm in awe of You, _   oh.

Gtr. 2

Verse

Gtr. 1: w/ Rhy. Fig. 1 (2 times)

2. What if I ig-nored the hand _ that fed me?   What if I for-got to con-fess? _

_____   What if I stum-bled down _ that moun-tain,   then would You love me less? ____

Gtr. 2

Gtr. 4 (elec.)

mf
w/ slight dist.

Lord, would You love me ___ less? _____

Gtr. 4: w/ Rhy. Fig. 1

Gtr. 2

What if I were ev - 'ry - one's last choice? ___ What if I mixed in with the rest? ___

___ What if I failed what I passed be - fore, _____ then would You love me less? __

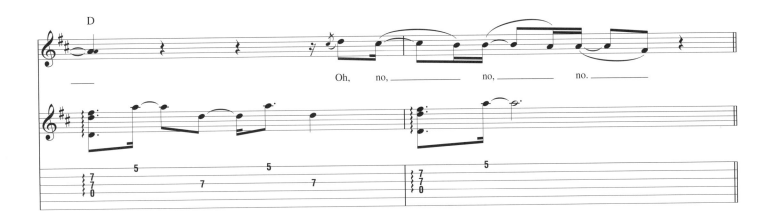

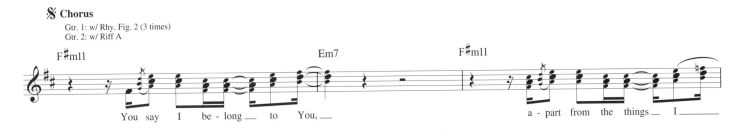

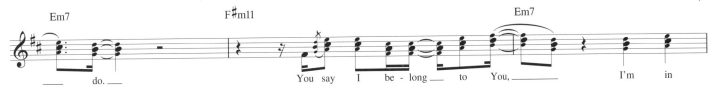

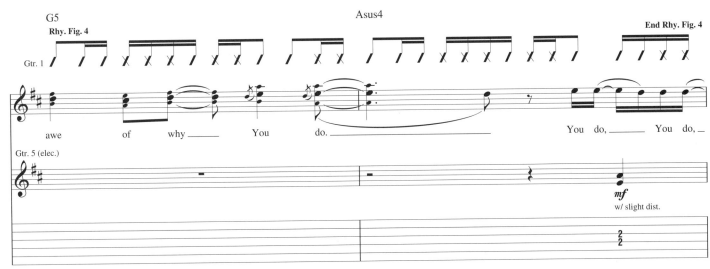

world that ___ keeps chang - in', ___ there's one thing ___ that I know _____

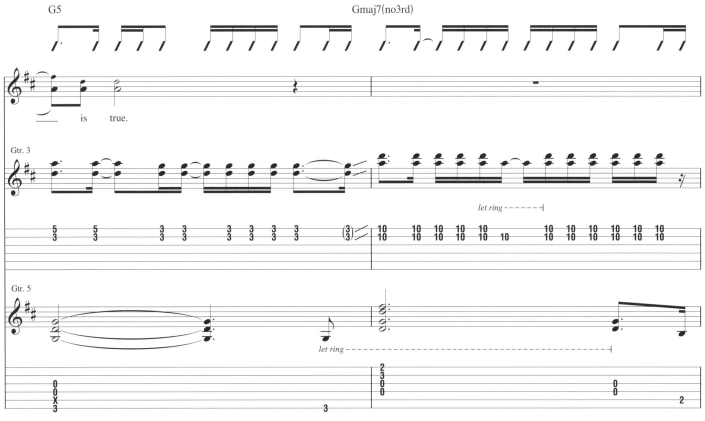

is true.

Your love ___ is stay - in', ___ there's noth - in' else ___ I'll hold on _____

_____ to. _____

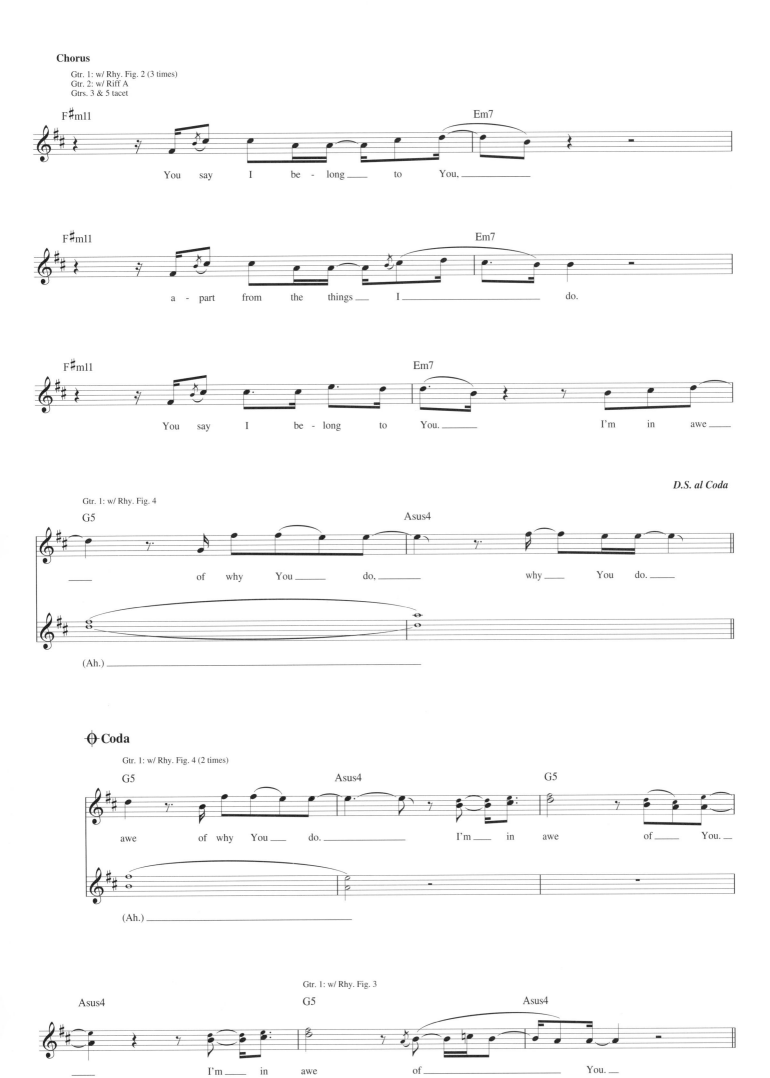

Outro

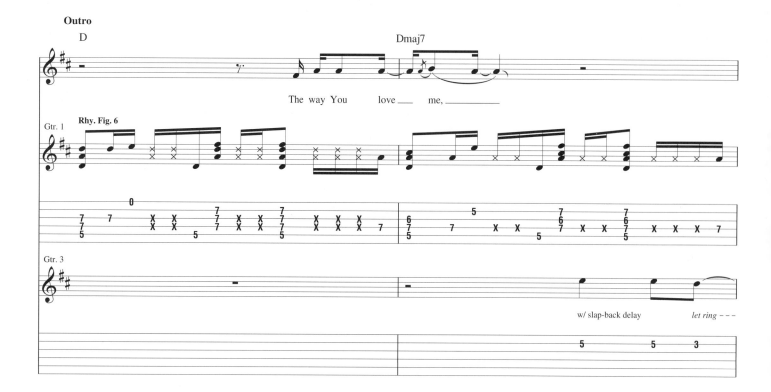

The way You love ___ me, _____

w/ slap-back delay   *let ring - - -*

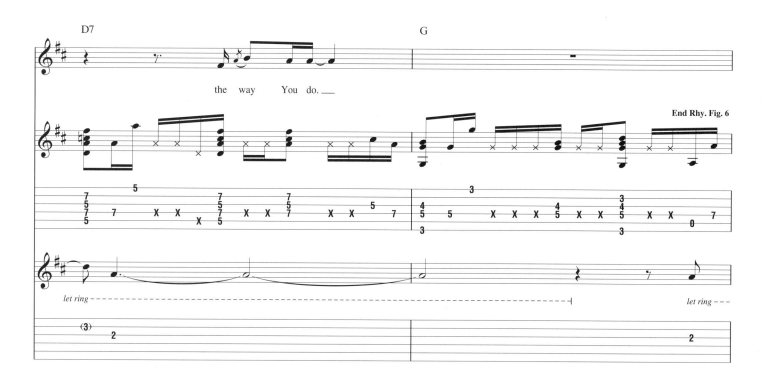

the way You do. ___

End Rhy. Fig. 6

let ring -   *let ring - - -*

Gtr. 1: w/ Rhy. Fig. 6

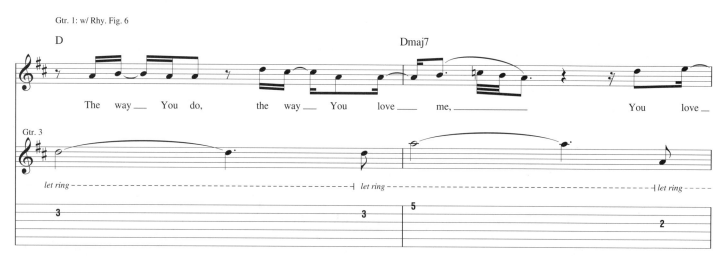

The way ___ You do,   the way ___ You love ___ me, _____   You love ___

let ring - - - - - - - - - - - - - *let ring - - - - - - - - -* *let ring - - - -*

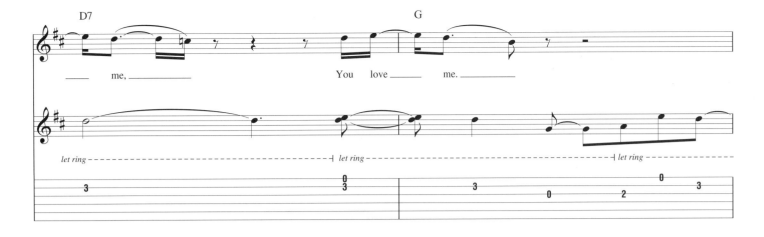

me,   You love   me.

Begin fade

Gtr. 1: w/ Rhy. Fig. 1 (till fade)

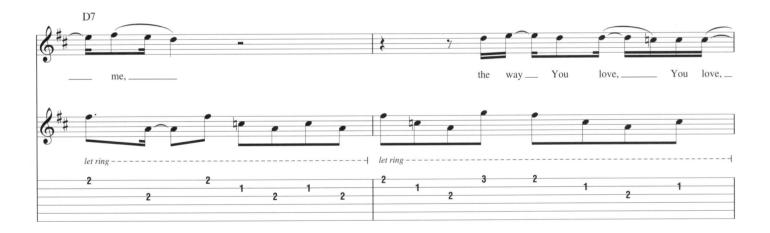

The way   You   do,   the way   You do,   the way You   love

me,   the way   You   love,   You love,

Fade out

You   love.

Guitar Notation Legend

Guitar music can be notated three different ways: on a *musical staff*, in *tablature*, and in *rhythm slashes*.

RHYTHM SLASHES are written above the staff. Strum chords in the rhythm indicated. Use the chord diagrams found at the top of the first page of the transcription for the appropriate chord voicings. Round noteheads indicate single notes.

THE MUSICAL STAFF shows pitches and rhythms and is divided by bar lines into measures. Pitches are named after the first seven letters of the alphabet.

TABLATURE graphically represents the guitar fingerboard. Each horizontal line represents a string, and each number represents a fret.

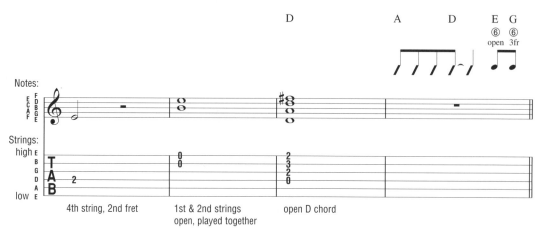

4th string, 2nd fret   1st & 2nd strings open, played together   open D chord

Definitions for Special Guitar Notation

HALF-STEP BEND: Strike the note and bend up 1/2 step.

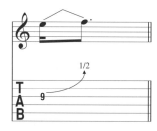

WHOLE-STEP BEND: Strike the note and bend up one step.

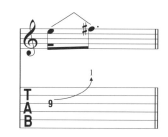

GRACE NOTE BEND: Strike the note and immediately bend up as indicated.

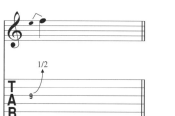

SLIGHT (MICROTONE) BEND: Strike the note and bend up 1/4 step.

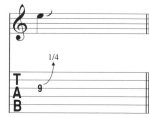

BEND AND RELEASE: Strike the note and bend up as indicated, then release back to the original note. Only the first note is struck.

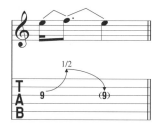

PRE-BEND: Bend the note as indicated, then strike it.

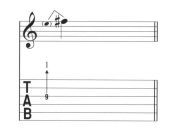

PRE-BEND AND RELEASE: Bend the note as indicated. Strike it and release the bend back to the original note.

UNISON BEND: Strike the two notes simultaneously and bend the lower note up to the pitch of the higher.

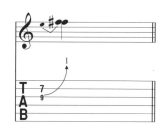

VIBRATO: The string is vibrated by rapidly bending and releasing the note with the fretting hand.

WIDE VIBRATO: The pitch is varied to a greater degree by vibrating with the fretting hand.

HAMMER-ON: Strike the first (lower) note with one finger, then sound the higher note (on the same string) with another finger by fretting it without picking.

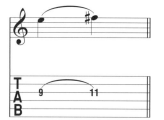

PULL-OFF: Place both fingers on the notes to be sounded. Strike the first note and without picking, pull the finger off to sound the second (lower) note.

LEGATO SLIDE: Strike the first note and then slide the same fret-hand finger up or down to the second note. The second note is not struck.

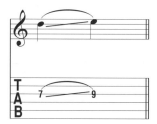

SHIFT SLIDE: Same as legato slide, except the second note is struck.

TRILL: Very rapidly alternate between the notes indicated by continuously hammering on and pulling off.

TAPPING: Hammer ("tap") the fret indicated with the pick-hand index or middle finger and pull off to the note fretted by the fret hand.

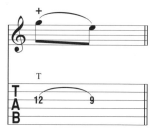

NATURAL HARMONIC: Strike the note while the fret-hand lightly touches the string directly over the fret indicated.

PINCH HARMONIC: The note is fretted normally and a harmonic is produced by adding the edge of the thumb or the tip of the index finger of the pick hand to the normal pick attack.

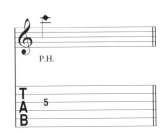

HARP HARMONIC: The note is fretted normally and a harmonic is produced by gently resting the pick hand's index finger directly above the indicated fret (in parentheses) while the pick hand's thumb or pick assists by plucking the appropriate string.

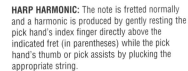
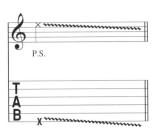

PICK SCRAPE: The edge of the pick is rubbed down (or up) the string, producing a scratchy sound.

MUFFLED STRINGS: A percussive sound is produced by laying the fret hand across the string(s) without depressing, and striking them with the pick hand.

PALM MUTING: The note is partially muted by the pick hand lightly touching the string(s) just before the bridge.

RAKE: Drag the pick across the strings indicated with a single motion.

TREMOLO PICKING: The note is picked as rapidly and continuously as possible.

ARPEGGIATE: Play the notes of the chord indicated by quickly rolling them from bottom to top.

VIBRATO BAR DIVE AND RETURN: The pitch of the note or chord is dropped a specified number of steps (in rhythm), then returned to the original pitch.

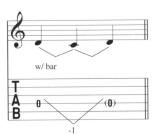

VIBRATO BAR SCOOP: Depress the bar just before striking the note, then quickly release the bar.

VIBRATO BAR DIP: Strike the note and then immediately drop a specified number of steps, then release back to the original pitch.

Additional Musical Definitions

(accent)	•	Accentuate note (play it louder).
(accent)	•	Accentuate note with great intensity.
(staccato)	•	Play the note short.
	•	Downstroke
	•	Upstroke
D.S. al Coda	•	Go back to the sign (℅), then play until the measure marked "*To Coda*," then skip to the section labelled "**Coda**."
D.C. al Fine	•	Go back to the beginning of the song and play until the measure marked "*Fine*" (end).

Rhy. Fig.	• Label used to recall a recurring accompaniment pattern (usually chordal).
Riff	• Label used to recall composed, melodic lines (usually single notes) which recur.
Fill	• Label used to identify a brief melodic figure which is to be inserted into the arrangement.
Rhy. Fill	• A chordal version of a Fill.
tacet	• Instrument is silent (drops out).
	• Repeat measures between signs.
	• When a repeated section has different endings, play the first ending only the first time and the second ending only the second time.

NOTE: Tablature numbers in parentheses mean:
1. The note is being sustained over a system (note in standard notation is tied), or
2. The note is sustained, but a new articulation (such as a hammer-on, pull-off, slide or vibrato) begins, or
3. The note is a barely audible "ghost" note (note in standard notation is also in parentheses).

More Christian Music
for Guitar

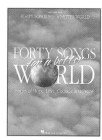

40 SONGS FOR A BETTER WORLD

40 songs with a message, including: All You Need Is Love • Bless the Beasts and Children • Colors of the Wind • Everything Is Beautiful • He Ain't Heavy...He's My Brother • I Am Your Child • Love Can Build a Bridge • What a Wonderful World • What the World Needs Now Is Love • You've Got a Friend • and more.
00702068 Easy Guitar with Notes & Tab.............$10.95

THE BEST OF STEVEN CURTIS CHAPMAN FOR EASY GUITAR

15 songs including: The Great Adventure • Heaven in the Real World • His Strength Is Perfect • I Will Be There • Move to This Life.

00702033 Easy Guitar with Notes & Tab.............$12.95

STEVEN CURTIS CHAPMAN FAVORITES

14 songs, including: Don't Let the Fire Die • Go There With You • Lord of the Dance • Runaway • When You Are a Soldier • and more.

00702073 Easy Guitar with Notes & Tab................$9.95

THE STEVEN CURTIS CHAPMAN GUITAR COLLECTION

12 of his most popular songs transcribed note-for-note for guitar, including: For the Sake of the Call • The Great Adventure • Heaven in the Real World • His Eyes • I Will Be Here • Lord of the Dance • More to This Life • Signs of Life • and more.
00690293 Guitar Transcriptions.........................$19.95

DC TALK – JESUS FREAK

Matching folio to this contemporary Christian band's crossover album. Songs include: Between You and Me • Jesus Freak • In the Light • Colored People • and more. Also includes photos.

00690184 Guitar Transcriptions.........................$19.95

CONTEMPORARY CHRISTIAN FAVORITES

20 great easy guitar arrangements of contemporary Christian songs, including: El Shaddai • Friends • He Is Able • I Will Be Here • In the Name of the Lord • In Christ Alone • Love in Any Language • Open My Heart • Say the Name • Thy Word • Via Dolorosa • and more.
00702006 Easy Guitar with Notes & Tab...............$9.95

FAVORITE HYMNS FOR EASY GUITAR

48 hymns, including: All Hail the Power of Jesus' Name • Amazing Grace • Be Thou My Vision • Blessed Assurance • Fairest Lord Jesus • I Love to Tell the Story • In the Garden • Let Us Break Bread Together • Rock of Ages • Were You There? • When I Survey the Wondrous Cross • and more.
00702041 Easy Guitar with Notes & Tab...............$9.95

GOSPEL FAVORITES FOR GUITAR

An amazing collection of 50 favorites, including: Amazing Grace • Did You Stop to Pray This Morning • He Lives • His Name Is Wonderful • How Great Thou Art • The King Is Coming • My God Is Real • Nearer, My God, To Thee • The Old Rugged Cross • Take My Hand, Precious Lord • Turn Your Radio On • Will the Circle Be Unbroken • and more.
00699374 Easy Guitar with Notes & Tab.............$14.95

BEST OF AMY GRANT

18 of her best arranged for easy guitar, including: Angels • Baby Baby • Big Yellow Taxi • Doubly Good to You • El Shaddai • Every Heartbeat • Find a Way • Good for Me • House of Love • Lead Me On • Lucky One • Tennessee Christmas • and more.
00702099 Easy Guitar with Notes & Tab...............$9.95

GREATEST HYMNS FOR GUITAR

48 hymns, including: Abide With Me • Amazing Grace • Be Still My Soul • Glory to His Name • In the Garden • and more.

00702116 Easy Guitar with Notes & Tab...............$7.95

MAKING SOME NOISE – TODAY'S MODERN CHRISTIAN ROCK

13 songs, including: Big House • Cup • Flood • God • Jesus Freak • Shine • Soulbait • and more.

00690216 Guitar Transcriptions.........................$14.95

TODAY'S CHRISTIAN FAVORITES

19 songs, including: Daystar • Find Us Faithful • Go West Young Man • God and God Alone • He Is Exalted • I Will Choose Christ • Jubilate • My Turn Now • A Perfect Heart • Revive Us, O Lord • and more.

00702042 Easy Guitar with Notes & Tab...............$8.95

FOR MORE INFORMATION, SEE YOUR LOCAL MUSIC DEALER, OR WRITE TO:

HAL•LEONARD® CORPORATION
7777 W. BLUEMOUND RD. P.O. BOX 13819 MILWAUKEE, WI 53213